W9-CLX-984

Careers for You Series

CAREERS FOR

CULTURE LOVERS

& Other Artsy Types

MARJORIE EBERTS
MARGARET GISLER

THIRD EDITION

New York Chicago San Francisco Lisbon London Madrid Mexico City
Milan New Delhi San Juan Seoul Singapore Sydney Toronto 2007

Library of Congress Cataloging-in-Publication Data

Eberts, Marjorie.
    Careers for culture lovers & other artsy types / by Marjorie Eberts,
Margaret Gisler.— 3rd ed.
        p. cm. — (McGraw-Hill careers for you series)
    ISBN 0-07-146777-7 (alk. paper)
    1. Arts—Vocational guidance—United States.   I. Title: Careers for
culture lovers and other artsy types.   II. Gisler, Margaret.   III. Title.

NX503.E24   2006
700.23′73—dc22   2006005970

· ·

To Anthony Poon, a very talented
architect and musician.
You are a true culture lover
who appreciates the arts.

1 2 3 4 5 6 7 8 9 0   DOC/DOC   0 9 8 7 6

ISBN-13: 978-0-07-146777-3
ISBN-10:   0-07-146777-7

McGraw-Hill books are available at special quantity discounts to use as premiums and
sales promotions, or for use in corporate training programs. For more information,
please write to the Director of Special Sales, Professional Publishing, McGraw-Hill,
Two Penn Plaza, New York, NY 10121-2298. Or contact your local bookstore.

This book is printed on acid-free paper.

Contents

· ·

Foreword

rt has the power to educate, entertain, and inspire us. Cultural events are a welcome respite from our daily routines, a chance to appreciate the creativity of others, to contemplate new ideas, to reevaluate our own perspectives on life. The fine arts offer more than recreation. They enhance the quality of our lives and contribute to our overall well-being.

For culture lovers, there's no greater pleasure than listening to a favorite symphony, going to the opera or ballet, or spending an afternoon admiring the work of a new painter. If you value the fine arts, you may also dream of finding a way to turn your avocation into a career.

Careers for Culture Lovers explores dozens of jobs behind the scenes in the fine arts. Music teachers, museum curators, choreographers, and set designers explain how they got started and describe the joys and frustrations of their jobs. They discuss the day-to-day work that keeps symphonies, theater companies, and art galleries in existence and allows the public to share the visions of talented composers, playwrights, and visual artists.

Culture lovers have a unique opportunity to provide that link between artist and audience. Through their work, teachers and arts administrators inspire future artists and create future audiences. Whatever their job descriptions, culture lovers use their skills in countless ways to cultivate in others the same appreciation for the arts that enriches their own lives.

CHAPTER ONE

Career Opportunities for Culture Lovers

Working with What Is Most Beautiful to the Senses and the Spirit

Culture is but the flowering of real education, and it is the training of the feeling, the tastes, and the manners that makes it so.
—Minnie Kellogg, Iroquois leader

A culture lover responds to what is pleasurable to the senses. You became a culture lover because you were exposed to what is beautiful in the world and developed a deep appreciation for it. It may have started as early as infancy, when you listened to and were enchanted by the music of Mozart and Brahms. Or perhaps you had a part in a school play or took dance lessons at an early age that awakened a love of theater or dance. In the same way, a course at school in art appreciation could have fostered a lifelong interest in art. Whatever your particular interest in the fine arts, it has become an important part of your life. And a career that involves this interest in some way is a perfect one for you.

Culture lovers are happiest when they are able to experience the fine arts. They savor time spent in art museums appreciating the creations of artists from Leonardo da Vinci to pop artist Andy Warhol. They relish the opportunity to view the arabesques and pirouettes of dancers as a story unfolds in a ballet. They feel themselves transformed as they listen to the music of a symphony orchestra performing a work by Beethoven, Tchaikovsky, or Mozart.

Culture lovers lean forward eagerly to view the stage when the curtain goes up for a play. It's not just art, dance, music, and theater that give great satisfaction to culture lovers; they enjoy viewing the amazing pictures of outstanding photographers, the imaginative buildings of world-renowned architects, and the magnificent jewelry of skilled artisans. Each work of art presents something special to the senses of culture lovers, whether it is the music they hear or the sculpture they view.

The magnetic pull of culture dominates the lives of culture lovers. They spend their money on paintings, prints, sculpture, tapes, CDs, and tickets to ballets, concerts, and theatrical productions. And the homes of culture lovers reflect their overwhelming interest in the arts, with music constantly filling the air, rooms decorated with works of art, and magazines and books on the different arts sitting on coffee and bedside tables.

Many culture lovers are not content to stand on the sidelines when it comes to enjoying the arts. They find time to be artists, musicians, singers, dancers, and actors. For some culture lovers, this means a part-time job, while for others it is a favorite avocation or recreation. Arts lovers spend hours of free time painting, sculpting, and making mosaics. Music lovers play in bands, orchestras, and chamber groups in their communities; sing in choral groups; or perform with the local opera company. And both singers and dancers often enjoy starring in musical productions, while actors put on makeup to do plays.

A Quick Look at Careers for Culture Lovers

Career opportunities as artists, musicians, singers, dancers, and actors are extremely limited. Successful careers in these areas require both talent and dedication. Few individuals can reach the stratospheric heights of international acclaim in the arts that Yo-Yo Ma, Luciano Pavarotti, Lucian Freud, Dame Judi Dench, Anthony Hopkins, and Mikhail Baryshnikov have attained. Furthermore, competition is so keen in the arts that only a few are able to earn a living entirely from their artistic endeavors. Fortunately, there's an amazing variety of jobs for culture lovers who wish to spend their work hours in jobs closely aligned to their own personal interests.

This book is dedicated to helping all culture lovers find jobs that let them work in areas they value. Here is a bird's-eye view of some of the careers that you will read about in this book.

Career Opportunities for Art Lovers

Wherever art is displayed, there are usually jobs that appeal to art lovers. Museums are especially appealing workplaces with their collections of paintings, sculpture, and other art forms. And depending on their size, museums need directors, curators, administrators, fund-raisers, financial managers, educators, gift shop employees, and guards. A job in an art gallery lets art lovers be part of the exciting world of buying and selling art. Jobs for art lovers are certainly not limited to museums and art galleries. Being an art critic for a newspaper or magazine allows art lovers to spend their days viewing and writing about art. Restorers and framers have hands-on jobs that actually let them handle art. And many jobs exist in public and private schools for those who wish to help people of all ages acquire skills in painting, drawing, sculpting, and other art forms.

Career Opportunities for Music Lovers

Music lovers with considerable expertise in music will find the greatest number of jobs associated with music as teachers. Teaching presents an opportunity to help fledgling musicians acquire basic skills and expert musicians refine their skills. Besides teaching, skilled musicians can find very satisfying jobs as music therapists, helping people in hospitals, mental health facilities, and nursing homes improve their health through music. Music lovers don't have to be skilled musicians, however, to find a wide variety of jobs with symphony orchestras, opera companies, choirs, and theatrical production companies. The larger a musical group, the greater the number of people required to handle administrative functions and backstage activities. Knowledgeable music lovers who like to write can find jobs as critics with newspapers and magazines, while those with technical skills can find jobs in the recording industry creating tapes, CDs, and videos. And, of course, there are jobs selling and repairing musical instruments as well as glamour jobs working with musical artists from Madonna to Billy Joel. Music lovers can even spend all their time with music as disc jockeys.

Career Opportunities for Dance Lovers

From ballroom dancing to viewing ballet and folk dance companies, dance is more popular than ever before, giving dance lovers many career opportunities. Dance companies offer many jobs to dance lovers who wish to help dancers prepare for and present performances. Behind every dance performance, there are choreographers, costume designers, wardrobe handlers, and stagehands. Dance lovers will also find some special jobs with dance companies, such as movement notators, who record as many details as are necessary to restage a dance performance. There are also reconstructors, who take these details and train the dance company to perform the dance according to the notations, and autographers, who put the notations in a form that can be distributed to all the dancers. A love of dance can also lead to a career as a dance therapist, restoring people to health through movement. Through teaching, dance lovers can share their love of dance with others. Both children and adults are eager to learn ballet, modern dance, folk dancing, and social dancing.

Career Opportunities for Theater Lovers

There's no business like show business, from Broadway productions to local dinner theaters. Wherever the lights go down and the curtains go up, there are jobs for theater lovers. For most theatrical productions, there are far more people working behind the scenes than there are actors on the stage. For all these productions, writers, directors, producers, publicists, business support staff, costume designers, dressers, set designers, hair stylists, prompters, sound and light engineers, and stagehands are required. Unfortunately, most theater jobs, except those of an administrative or clerical nature, end with the final curtain of a production. Only jobs with the League of Resident Theaters (LORT) are year-round jobs. Most theater lovers are freelancers who move from one show to another.

More Career Opportunities for Culture Lovers

Literature, photography, interior design, architecture, furniture, textiles, and jewelry can also be included within the broad world of fine arts. The creators of these aesthetically pleasing art forms require many assistants to produce and sell their finished works. Culture lovers interested in these arts can find jobs in museums, galleries, and stores. For example, working in an antique store can be a wonderful opportunity to be surrounded by beautiful and historical objects.

A vast amount of money is distributed each year by governmental bodies, corporations, individuals, and foundations that support the arts. Decisions have to be made about which arts groups will receive this money. Culture lovers can find a variety of challenging jobs in the organizations that disburse these funds.

Dream Jobs for Culture Lovers

When culture lovers read want ads in newspapers or magazines or look for positions on the Internet, they are always searching for jobs that will allow them to spend more time working in areas that are closely tied to their interests. The following position descriptions would surely capture the attention of many arts lovers.

DANCE THERAPIST

Full-time position with prestigious long-term care facility. Competitive pay and benefits.

MUSIC EDUCATOR

Private school seeks teachers for child groups, birth to age seven. Must sing on pitch, follow rhythm. Will train the rest. Flexible hours and excellent pay.

SENIOR ASSOCIATE DIRECTOR

Local university seeks individual to assist the director of development in the design, implementation, and management of a program of activities to generate philanthropic gift support to the Museum of Art. Specific responsibility for segments of major gift prospect research, cultivation, solicitation, and stewardship activities required for the anticipated capital campaign. Bachelor's degree required, as is at least four years of experience.

FULL-TIME SALES REPRESENTATIVE

Here is an exciting opportunity to join a world-renowned international retailer of exquisite jewelry and fine merchandise. Our Boston location is currently interviewing for sales professionals. Qualified applicants must be friendly, diligent individuals with a high degree of enthusiasm and professionalism. Candidates must have one year of related experience.

Job Qualifications

Culture lovers appreciate objects and experiences that arouse their senses. A love of culture, while essential, is not sufficient qualification for obtaining many jobs in the arts. Specialized training or academic degrees are required for many of these careers. For example, culture lovers wanting to help people through music or dance therapy must combine college courses in music with extensive work in the behavioral and biological sciences. Quite often in the arts arena, a master's degree is a prerequisite for even being considered for a position. And there are many jobs where holding a double master's degree or a doctorate is necessary to obtain a specific job. Fortunately, a considerable part of the course work allows most culture lovers to gain more and more knowledge of their favorite art forms. And culture lovers seeking careers associated with the arts realize that they must have the best training and education in order to meet the challenges that lie ahead in their careers.

Starting Your Career

Because working closely with art, music, dance, theater, and other fine arts is so immensely satisfying to culture lovers, there is considerable competition for many entry-level positions. Jobs in museums and with symphony orchestras and theatrical groups are especially competitive. Besides requiring the appropriate educational background, entry-level jobs typically go to those with some experience. The best way to garner this experience is by working as a volunteer or intern, which allows you to explore a career in a specific area as well as network with individuals who may know about job openings.

Culture lovers can find out about positions in the arts through advertisements in newspapers and magazines associated with the different arts. In addition, many jobs can be found by using the job search capabilities of the Internet. If you would like a job with a particular organization, such as a symphony orchestra or a foundation, you should explore the organization's website as many include job listings.

Where the Jobs Are

For many culture lovers, relocation is the name of the game when they are looking for employment in the arts, since the largest number and variety of jobs are found in major metropolitan areas. Nevertheless, it is not essential for culture lovers to seek employment in just a few large cities. Scattered across the country in communities of every size there are jobs for arts lovers. For example, jobs in education will be found in even the smallest towns where culture lovers can teach in schools or give lessons in their homes.

Further Reading

A deeper appreciation of the arts emerges as people learn more about them. In fact, a great part of being a culture lover is studying and nourishing the mind with beauty in its many forms. There are several excellent guides that can help you become better acquainted with the different arts.

Art

Bjelajac, David. *American Art: A Cultural History.* Upper Saddle River, NJ: Prentice Hall, 2004.

Craven, Wayne. *American Art: History and Culture.* New York: McGraw-Hill, 2002.

Janson, Anthony F. *History of Art.* Upper Saddle River, NJ: Prentice Hall, 2004.

Kleiner, Fred S., and Christin J. Mamiya. *Gardner's Art Through the Ages*. Florence, KY: Wadsworth Publishing, 2004.

Perry, Gill, and Paul Wood, eds. *Themes in Contemporary Art (Art of the 20th Century)*. New Haven, CT: Yale University Press, 2004.

Music

Douglas, Nigel. *The Joy of Opera*. London: Trafalgar Square Books, 2005.

Hoffer, Charles. *Music Listening Today*. Florence, KY: Wadsworth Publishing, 2002.

Kamien, Roger. *Music: An Appreciation*. New York: McGraw-Hill, 2003.

McGee, Richard L., and Joan B. McGee. *Music to Your Ears: An Introduction to Classical Music*. Dubuque, IA: Kendall Hunt Publishing Company, 2003.

Yudkin, Jeremy, *Understanding Music*. Upper Saddle River, NJ: Prentice Hall, 2004.

Dance

Carter, Alexandra, ed. *Rethinking Dance History: A Reader*. New York: Routledge, 2004.

Dils, Ann, and Ann Cooper, eds. *Moving History/Dancing Cultures: A Dance History Reader*. Delaware, OH: Wesleyan University Press, 2001.

Ellison, Nancy. *The Book of Ballet: Learning and Appreciating the Secrets of Dance*. New York: Universe Publishing, 2003.

Lee, Carol. *Ballet in Western Culture: A History of Its Origins and Evolution*. New York: Routledge, 2002.

Reynolds, Nancy, and Malcolm McCormick. *No Fixed Points: Dance in the Twentieth Century*. New Haven, CT: Yale University Press, 2003.

Theater

Brockett, Oscar G., and Franklin J. Hildy. *History of the Theatre.* Boston: Allyn & Bacon, 2002.

Brown, John Russell, ed. *The Oxford Illustrated History of Theatre.* Oxford, UK: Oxford University Press, 2001.

Jones, John Bush. *Our Musicals, Ourselves: A Social History of the American Musical Theater.* Lebanon, NH: University Press of New England, 2004.

Shakespeare, William. *The Essential Shakespeare: 12 Great Plays.* Mineola, NY: Dover Publications, 2004.

Smith, Helaine L. *Masterpieces of Classic Greek Drama.* Westport, CT: Greenwood Press, 2005.

CHAPTER TWO

Career Opportunities for Art Lovers

Working with Paintings, Sculpture, and Other Art Forms in Many Settings

The excellence of every art is its intensity, capable of making all disagreeables evaporate, from their being in close relationship with beauty and truth.
—John Keats, letter to G. and T. Keats

Art is what appeals most to many culture lovers. From the earliest times, art has satisfied people's need for an aesthetic experience. They have used art to remember important events as well as enjoyed its myriad shapes and colors and mediums. It is not always easy to express one's satisfaction with art in words. Nevertheless, for art lovers, art is one part of their lives they value most highly.

People who love art can lose themselves in a painting, sculpture, mosaic, mural, or drawing. Not only do they appreciate seeing the works of well-known artists, they also enjoy seeing the efforts of those just beginning to exercise their talents. A deep satisfaction can be found in studying art for pleasure or learning how

11

the artist felt about subjects such as religion, family, and social justice.

Fortunately for art lovers, the enjoyment of art does not have to be a leisure-time activity; there are many jobs that let them spend their workdays surrounded by art. They can have extremely satisfying careers working in art museums or galleries. Jobs with newspapers and magazines as art commentators or critics give art lovers a chance to share their opinions of works of art with others. Art lovers also have the opportunity to educate both children and adults on artistic techniques and the history of art as teachers. In fact, a variety of jobs exist for those who wish to work in some way with art.

Art Museums—Paradise for Art Lovers

According to the American Association of Museums (AAM), a museum is an organized and permanent nonprofit institution, essentially educational or aesthetic in purpose, with professional staff, that owns and uses tangible objects, cares for them, and exhibits them to the public on some regular schedule. While this is an all-purpose definition, the word *art* in *art museum* indicates that these museums care for and exhibit works of art. Art museums vary greatly in their specialties. An art museum may show works of art from ancient times to the present in many mediums, as the Metropolitan Museum of Art in New York City and the Art Institute of Chicago do. Or an art museum may specialize in the art of one period, artist, or medium. For example, the Museum of Modern Art in New York City is devoted to the collection and exhibition of modern art; the Asian Art Museum of San Francisco concentrates on Asian art from many eras. No matter what specialty interests an art lover, there is probably an art museum devoted to that interest. It is possible for art lovers to find jobs at museums devoted solely to craft and folk art, Native American art and artifacts, or French Impressionist collections. By reading the annual *Official Museum Directory*, art lovers can learn just about everything they need to know about individual museums. The directory has information about museum personnel; areas of collections; and the nature, size, and scope of each of the facilities listed. The directory is available in some public and university libraries, and more can be learned about it by visiting the website at www.officialmuseumdir.com.

The Louvre, founded in Paris in 1793, is generally considered the first real art museum. In the United States, it was not until the end of the 1800s that the number of art museums began to grow rapidly. Today, art lovers will find major art museums in large cities like New York, Boston, Minneapolis, San Francisco, Los Angeles, Chicago, and Philadelphia. They can also find art museums scattered across the country in towns as diverse as Helena, Montana; Akron, Ohio; Utica, New York; Anchorage, Alaska; Andover, Massachusetts; and Sarasota, Florida.

How Museums Work

The purpose of museums is to collect, preserve, research, exhibit, and interpret objects of lasting value for the public, according to the AAM. Museums obtain their collections by buying, trading with other museums, and receiving gifts. The museum staff keeps an accurate record of every object in the museum. The staff repairs and restores damaged objects and employs scientific techniques to protect the collection from deterioration. Most museums store the greater part of their collections for scholarly investigation and only exhibit their choicest objects for their patrons. Museums also offer a wide variety of educational activities, including courses, lectures, publications, and guide services.

Career Options in Art Museums

Staff members are needed for a wide variety of positions in art museums—from designing exhibits, soliciting funds, and guarding collections to conducting research, keeping financial records, and sweeping floors. In large museums, staff members often have duties in a closely defined area, such as curator of Egyptian art.

However, in small museums, employees need to be jacks-of-all-trades, capable of handling diverse tasks, from training docents to cataloging objects. In all art museums, there is a need for people with sound business backgrounds to run the financial side of the organization. Employees are also needed to handle clerical and maintenance tasks.

Because art museums are so very different in size, budgets, and collections, the following job descriptions of key personnel provide the basic functions of each position.

- **Director:** carries out the policy of the board of the museum and is the manager of all functions of the museum. All staff positions report to the director.
- **Curator:** responsible for the care and interpretation of all objects in the museum and for research on the collections. The curator recommends acquisitions and removals of artworks from the collection. Duties may include organizing exhibitions.
- **Conservator:** scientifically analyzes museum objects to prevent deterioration and repairs them when necessary. The conservator is responsible for keeping objects in the collection at the proper temperature and humidity and protected from pests, pollution, and harmful light exposure.
- **Exhibits Designer:** turns the ideas of the museum's curators and educators into drawings or scale models for permanent, temporary, or traveling exhibits. The designer may also be responsible for setting up the exhibit.
- **Registrar:** in charge of cataloging objects in the collection and maintaining proper documents, such as insurance, copyright, and reproduction rights. Responsibilities also include the packing, unpacking, shipping, and storing of art objects, plus the handling of customs problems.
- **Educator:** develops, implements, and supervises the formal and informal teaching programs of the museum with the goal of increasing the public's understanding of the art

collection. Duties can include in-service instruction
for docents, workshops for museum faculty, and establishing lecture series, film programs, tours, special events,
seminars, and school programs.

- **Development Officer:** in charge of raising money for
the museum through the solicitation of individuals and
corporations for donations of money; this person also
plans, coordinates, and implements all fund-raising programs. Supervising the development staff is an additional
responsibility.
- **Membership Officer:** responsible for attracting new
members, retaining existing membership in the museum,
and organizing special events and programs for the members. Duties can include the maintenance of membership
records.

The American Association of Museums has also identified the
following positions as museum-related jobs:

accountant	gardener/landscaper
archivist	graphic artist
artist	guard
attorney	historian
audiovisual technician	instructor
building superintendent	librarian
business manager	maintenance worker
clerk	model maker
computer specialist	personnel director
controller	public relations specialist
curatorial assistant	publications director
editor	research assistant
electrician	sales shop manager
filmmaker	secretary
food service manager	volunteer manager

Job Qualifications

For museum jobs, especially those actively involved in working in some way with the art collection, the key word in getting a job is *experience*. The two best ways to get needed experience are by participating in an internship program and serving as a volunteer. Visit the museums that interest you online to see what opportunities each offers.

For art lovers aspiring to positions as directors, curators, educators, registrars, conservators, and librarians, master's degrees in museum studies, the museum's specialization, or in specific work areas are generally expected. For some prestigious museums, only applicants with doctoral degrees are considered. Bachelor's degrees in business or arts administration are normally required for those seeking employment on the business side of art museums in such jobs as business manager, development officer, personnel director, and public relations specialist.

Being affiliated with museum or professional associations is a plus for those seeking jobs in art museums. And since almost all jobs in museums require interaction with the public, from the guard talking to museum patrons to the director speaking to the board of the museum, good communication skills are necessary.

Salaries

Salaries of art museum workers are similar to those working in other museums. Employees at major metropolitan museums usually earn considerably more than those at small museums in towns or rural areas. Salaries also depend on an individual's level of education and years of experience. Many individuals get their first positions in museums as unpaid interns or volunteers.

Table 1 shows the mean salaries of employees in both the largest museums, with operating budgets of more than $20 million, and smaller ones, with budgets under $1 million, from a survey by the Association of Art Museum Directors.

TABLE 1. Museum Salaries

POSITION	LARGE MUSEUM	SMALL MUSEUM
Director	$369,458	$100,000
Chief Curator	$132,755	$52,780
Senior Curator	$91,545	$46,965
Curatorial Assistant	$33,572	$25,390

Source: Association of Art Museum Directors

A Look at Job Opportunities

Jobs in museums are attractive to art lovers, which results in keen competition for certain positions, as many applicants have the necessary training and subject knowledge and there are few openings. For example, candidates for curator positions may have to work part-time, as an intern, or even as a volunteer assistant curator or research associate, after completing a formal education. Applicants for archivist positions have the best opportunities if they have highly specialized training, such as master's degrees in both library science and history, with a concentration in archives or records management and extensive computer skills. The best job outlook is for conservators who are graduates of a conservation program and willing to relocate. Art lovers who want to work in museums also need to understand that jobs in museums are often subject to funding cuts during recessions or periods of budget tightening, reducing the demand for new employees. Overall, employment in museums is expected to increase as fast as the average for all occupations through the year 2012.

Director of a Smaller Art Museum

No one determines what the character of an art museum will be more than the director. In Saint Paul, Minnesota, Jim Czarniecki served as the director of the Minnesota Museum of American Art and determined that this museum would be people oriented. Under his leadership, the Museum School offered a formal instructional program in studio art and art history. These classes were scheduled to accommodate the variety of student needs and lifestyles: after-work classes for the downtown work crowd; traditional evening hours; and weekend workshops. Although the museum is people oriented, important research in American art is not neglected. The staff is working on redefining American art and, through its research, is bringing out what has been ignored or repressed in the past.

Like most art museum directors, Jim had the responsibility for hiring and training support staff. Although the Minnesota Museum of American Art was then considered a small or mid-sized museum, it had a staff of twenty-six full-time employees, fifteen part-time employees, and a faculty of twenty-five part-time teachers in the Museum School. One of Jim's duties as director was to interpret the board's policy for the staff and to design programs that would help the staff carry out this policy. Vision is required in the director's job: Jim was involved in setting goals and objectives for the museum to reach in the next three to five years. He was also the chief representative for the museum in the Twin Cities community, which required frequent dialog with community leaders in business and government.

Every day is different for the director of a museum. Jim spent 60 to 70 percent of his time working on all facets of the museum's campaign to raise $20 million to build a new facility. Much of his fund-raising time was spent talking to members of the board of trustees, donors, and key volunteers. One very appealing aspect of working in a museum this size is that directors are able to stay close to art. Jim was able to curate a show and be intimately involved in building the art collection.

Career Path. Although Jim was always interested in art and even took oil painting lessons in elementary school, he certainly did not expect to have a career in the arts. During high school, his interest was aeronautics, and he only took one art course. After graduation, Jim spent one year in Antwerp, Belgium, with the American Field Service program. During this year, his interest in art, especially photography, was reawakened. In college, Jim's major was physics, but he spent more time in the photography lab than the physics lab, as he was a photographer for both the newspaper and the yearbook. After graduation, jobs in physics were hard to find, and Jim finally determined that his interest was really photography and art. He elected to look for a job as a photographer.

Between interviews for photography jobs, Jim walked into the personnel office of the Art Institute of Chicago without an appointment and by the end of the day had a job with the Department of Education writing gallery guides and organizing a film and lecture series for a photography exhibition. Besides working at the Art Institute, Jim also enrolled part-time in classes to continue his education in art, especially in photography and filmmaking. Within two years, he was promoted to the position of supervisor of all public programs in the education department. His mentor at the museum allowed him to expand his knowledge of photography even further by letting him take time away from his job to do two internships in photography.

After three years of supervising programs at the Art Institute, the Ringling Museum of Art in Sarasota, Florida, offered Jim the job of director of education. He saw the job as an excellent opportunity to try out his ideas of making art more accessible to the public. He succeeded in bringing art to the people by establishing affiliate organizations with other museums in other cities and forming chapters of citizen volunteer groups that sponsored one or two exhibitions each year.

Jim's success with the Ringling program brought him an offer from patrons of the Mississippi Art Association to establish an art museum in Jackson and to serve as its director. The association wanted someone who would create a museum that was very responsive to the public. Operating from an antebellum house with galleries in two parlors, Jim was able to help design the new museum and get it operating in eighteen months. Seven years later, the Minnesota Museum of American Art asked Jim to serve as director.

Human Resources, Administrative, and Events Manager

At the Minnesota Museum of American Art, Carey Matthews is one of the full-time employees who has several responsibilities, just like most of the other employees do. One of them is human resources, where she handles staff insurance, benefits, and interpersonnel relations. Carey also handles the administrative work of the museum—a job she describes as being similar to an office manager in a business. Her job includes overseeing accounts receivable and accounts payable, monitoring the cash flow, maintaining office equipment, and ordering supplies. She also works with the director on many tasks, including making some executive-level decisions for the museum. Carey particularly enjoys working as events manager because it allows her to be creative as she manages all aspects of events, especially parties. She works with the museum staff to make sure events tie in with exhibits. One thing that Carey particularly likes about this job is its diversity. It also is appealing because, as an art lover, her workplace is a museum with ever-changing displays of art.

Career Path. Carey graduated from college with a bachelor's degree in acting; however, she had also taken many art courses when she was younger. Moving to Minnesota gave her the opportunity to take part in the very active theater scene in the Minneapolis–St. Paul area. While trying to get acting jobs, just like most beginning actors, she had to get a full-time position. At first, Carey was an administrative assistant at a property management company, and then she took a similar position with a for-profit company that produced bicycle rides that raised money for non-profit AIDS organizations.

When this job ended, she went online to a website listing jobs at nonprofit organizations, which considerably narrowed her search, as she knew that she wanted to work for an organization with a mission she found important. She submitted her resume to the Minnesota Museum of American Art and was called in for an interview. She did not have any connections at the museum or prior museum experience, two things that often get your foot in the door in such a narrow, sought-after field. Carey believes that she got this job not only because of her interest in art, but also because she had the broad-based, useful skills the museum was seeking.

Career Advice. Carey points out that you can come in at the bottom in a large museum and work your way up because bigger museums have more tiered positions, depending on your education and experience. At smaller museums, she says that it is more difficult to change jobs, but you often take on more duties that expand your job description and skill set.

Curators—Guardians of Art

Beyond researching and interpreting the art in their care and arranging exhibitions, curators are the keepers of the art heritage that resides in museums. The number of curators working in an art museum is closely tied to the size of the museum. In a large museum such as the Fine Arts Museums of San Francisco, which comprises the de Young and Legion of Honor museums, you will find curators of such collections as ancient art, European decorative art, European paintings, works on paper, American painting and decorative arts, African art, art of Oceania, art of the Americas, and textiles. The typical curatorial career path is outlined in the following diagram.

A similar career path is found in mid-sized museums; however, in very small museums there may not be any specifically named curatorial positions, as the director may also serve as the curator.

Curator of the Textile Department

Melissa Leventon was the curator of the textile department of the Fine Arts Museums of San Francisco. In this position, she had the mandate of caring for fifteen thousand textiles and costumes from all over the world. To help in this task, she had an associate curator. Although her department did not have a formal internship program, unpaid interns frequently worked in the department when a suitable project arose. Melissa advises art lovers who are interested in being a curator to get a taste of what it is like by serving as interns or volunteers.

A curator's job is a multifaceted one in which the day's tasks vary. Melissa was involved in researching, writing, and cataloging, which meant spending considerable time on the computer. Melissa also had the responsibility of looking for new pieces to add to the collection and raising funds. Like most curators, she had the challenge of coming up with ideas for exhibitions. This was a big task in her department as there were usually two new exhibits in the costume gallery, two in the ethnographic textiles gallery, and one in the tapestries gallery every year. Plus, every two or three years, Melissa set up a big exhibition. One was an outstanding exhibition—The Mystery of the Dead Sea Scrolls—that was widely acclaimed. Arranging for a new exhibit can take from six to thirty-six months, while installing the exhibit may require from one day to three weeks. It is important for prospective curators to understand that besides being involved with art in some way, this job also requires considerable administrative work.

Career Path. Melissa has always been fascinated by what people wear; she made a lot of costumes for theatrical productions in high school. When she entered the job market, she was well prepared with a bachelor's degree in English and a master's in the history of dress. Her first position was as a curatorial assistant in costumes and textiles at the Museum of London. Then she became an assistant curator for the textile department at the Fine Arts Museums of San Francisco before becoming curator. Today, she is self-employed.

Conservators—Advocates for Works of Art

Conservators are the experts who are interested primarily in the welfare of works of art. Their job is to prevent deterioration and repair paintings, sculptures, books, textiles, rugs, tapestries, picture frames, porcelains, other fine works of art and cultural properties. Conservators usually have a specialty, since the problems to be resolved in caring for works of art are so diverse that no individual can be an expert in restoring all kinds of art. Preserving a two-thousand-year-old carving found in the ocean and preserving a fifteenth-century porcelain vase are two very different tasks.

Educational Requirements. Becoming a conservator is a long process, whether art lovers do it through a formal school program or through an apprenticeship that lasts a minimum of five years and usually extends to eight years. There are no undergraduate programs that give bachelor's degrees in conservation. However, it is possible to take technical studies at the undergraduate level and then enter an apprentice or master's program. The first step in the academic approach is to get a bachelor's degree, usually in art history, which should be coupled with undergraduate courses in chemistry, archeology, or studio art. Knowing a foreign language is also helpful. Obtaining a master's degree in a conservator's program in some areas of study is quite difficult because of the limited number of schools and limited number of applicants accepted into programs. Many students have to wait two to three years to enter a master's program in this area. During that time, they are expected to gain experience working for a conservator. After graduation, they must serve in an internship. Check your library for a listing of schools offering conservation programs. You can request career information from:

American Institute for Conservation of Historic and
   Artistic Works
1717 K Street NW, Suite 200
Washington, DC 20006
http://aic.stanford.edu

A Conservator of Fine Art

Larger museums have laboratories where conservators work. Smaller museums either tap into the resources of the larger museums or use private conservators. Scott M. Haskins is a conservator who directs a fine art conservation laboratory. His area of expertise in conservation is fine paintings and works of art on paper. Scott's clients include museums of all types: city, state, and federal governments; historical societies; corporations with large art holdings; and holders of private collections. Scott trained in Italy and obtained the equivalent of a master's degree in fine arts conservation, followed by a one-year internship.

In his conservation work, Scott is involved in such tasks as taking water stains out of a seventeenth-century drawing, cleaning and repairing rips in paintings, taking acid stains out of watercolors, repairing and preserving frames, and stopping the deterioration of paintings and works of art on paper. He is interested in every aspect of an artwork's welfare. He sees that it is shipped and stored correctly and advises clients on how to prevent light and pollution damage to paintings. Art scholars also use him as a consultant in determining the authenticity of works of art. He was able to tell one scholar that a work of art supposedly by Goya could not be genuine because the whites used in the painting were not invented until 1927.

Scott also has administrative responsibilities. He supervises a conservator and an apprentice with a master's degree in art history and sets up the daily work schedule for the laboratory. A very important part of his job is making sure that all work done on art in the laboratory is carefully documented. In addition, he spends time talking to clients and prospective clients.

Museums seek these highly trained professionals for staff positions or as consultants. Because so much still has to be learned about how to conserve works of art, employment opportunities are also good for conservation scientists who research the effects of such things as pollution, humidity, and lighting on works of art.

Exhibit Designers—Experts in Displaying Art

Exhibit designers do more than prepare works of art for display in a museum; they also prepare the space to hold the works of art. The designers are responsible for lighting, wall colors, support graphics for the works of art, audiovisual materials, traffic flow, and security for an exhibit. They must also see that the exhibit tells a story with a beginning, middle, and end.

Sherman O'Hara is the chief exhibits designer at the Indianapolis Museum of Art, in charge of the more than thirty new exhibits featured in the museum each year. He works directly on the installation of eight exhibits a year. His work year is rather like show business—"another opening, another show." Each installation begins with a curator telling him or one of the designers on his staff what the story line of the exhibit will be. In many museums, the curator, exhibits designer, and educator plan the exhibit story together. The next step is for the exhibits designer to plan the actual exhibit, which must be approved by the curator. Then a drawing of the exhibit is made. The final step is the installation of the exhibit. This is done by a team including the designer, a lighting technician, someone who mounts the paintings, and other necessary technicians. At times, the museum exhibits "packaged" shows that already come with a story line. In this case, the designer tailors the exhibit to fit the space.

Sherman has a staff of seven in his department. Two of these people are exhibits designers. When the schedule of exhibits is published for the year, the designers choose or are assigned to the exhibits they will do during the year. In the past ten years, the career of exhibits designer has become more professional. There is now a standing committee of exhibits designers on the board of the American Association of Museums. And designers now have their own professional organization—the National Association of Museum Exhibitors. There is no specific course work that is recognized as preparation for this career. Most designers have a bachelor's or master's degree in fine arts with an architectural or design background. As this profession has become more disciplined, there are now opportunities for internships in this area in museums. Sherman now has one intern each year. Being an intern is an excellent way to get experience in this area.

Being the chief exhibits designer means that Sherman is responsible for a considerable amount of paperwork. He manages his department's budget, handles correspondence, and orders materials. He must also plan and attend meetings and make sure that exhibits are installed on schedule.

Career Path. Sherman originally considered a career in accounting and actually graduated as a business major. After graduation, he changed his mind and went to a school of design for postgraduate work. Then he and a partner started a space design business. After they sold the business, he traveled and then took a job at the Indianapolis Museum of Art as chief exhibits designer—the same job he holds today.

Educator—a Performance Arts Coordinator

Anna Thompson learned about a position at the Indianapolis Museum of Art through a newspaper advertisement. The ad read:

> The Indianapolis Museum of Art has an opening for a full-time music performance arts coordinator. We are seeking an experienced educator with a background in music and/or music and film to research, develop, and implement the music, film, and performance arts programs for the museum. Many programs are designed in conjunction with educational programming for the permanent collection and special exhibitions. Concerts and film series are presented on weekends and evenings. Master's degree in music or related fields is highly desirable. Three to five years university or high school teaching experience or equivalent. Background in film study or art history also desirable. Strong oral, written, communication, and organizational skills required.

Anna had been a school music teacher for three years, held an advanced degree in library science, and had experience in organizing educational programs at the library and making arrangements for a meeting of the National Conference of Music Librarians, which qualified her for the position. She applied and was hired. Her job involved dealing with several media—art, music, and film. Anna researched and developed programs related to specific art exhibits. She selected films for the summer film series. In addition, she put together programs that were sent out to the schools. When the museum's new pavilion opened, Anna commissioned a work by a composer to reflect the artist's work in the exhibition. In this job, she also wrote grant proposals to obtain funds for the performing arts programs. In carrying out her job, she worked closely with the museum's curators.

Coordinator of Youth and Family Programs

All museums today are trying to interest young children in art. One way to do this is by establishing programs just for families. Tariq Robinson is coordinator of the youth and family programs at the Indianapolis Museum of Art, which are designed for families with children between the ages of five and ten. The families attending the museum's programs are not all traditional families. Some could be part of groups such as Big Brothers and Big Sisters.

Once a month between October and June, Tariq arranges every part of a program that runs between eleven and four. He selects a theme such as color and shape or movement and art. Then he always tries to reach the children by selecting something familiar that is tied to a museum exhibit. For example, when the museum had a robots display (the familiar) in which the robots responded to movement and voice, he tied it to acquainting them with avant-garde animation films. Also, there may be such elements in a program as gallery tours, theater performances, and art lessons.

Career Path. Tariq was not always involved in the arts even though he had always been an avid museum visitor. He graduated with a business degree and pursued a business career only to discover that working in the corporate world was not for him. He went back to college at the Herron School of Art and found an internship that gave him a picture of what it was like to work in a museum. His first task was to work with the curator of African art in setting up an exhibit for a community center. This involved research, labeling pieces, and setting up the display. The internship led to a full-time paid position at the museum coordinating the annual Africafest event. Budget cuts eliminated this program, but Tariq continued to work at the museum helping other curators set up exhibitions. This work led to his present position.

Tariq sees himself continuing to work at a museum. He loves the creativity involved in the job, working with art, and all the fun of doing this work.

Human Resources Manager at the Walker Art Center

Almost every member of the administrative staff at the Walker Art Center in Minneapolis, Minnesota, is an artist who brings an artist's sensitivity to his or her position. Wendy Lane, a former human resources manager at the museum, is no exception. Art is so important to her that she lives in a studio with both living and work space and meets once a month with other artists to critique each other's work.

In her job as human resources manager, her primary responsibility was recruitment. When a new staff member was needed, she wrote the job description and then saw that the opening was publicized. This involved sending the posting to about 350 arts and service organizations as well as placing ads. Wendy handled the response by reviewing resumes and working with the supervisor of the open position to decide who would be interviewed. The supervisor did the initial interview, and Wendy did the final interview before they got together to make a decision.

The demand for positions at the very prestigious Walker Art Center is huge. Hundreds will apply for every position, especially since many artists want to work at art museums. Just having a background in art is not a sufficient qualification for most positions. Applicants generally need to have bachelor's degrees, with advanced degrees preferable for many positions.

Besides her recruitment responsibilities, Wendy was in charge of new employee orientation. She talked to new employees about the museum's policies and procedures and signed them up for benefits. And when an employee left, she would do the exit interview and the paperwork on the termination.

As part of her job, she wrote the policy and procedures booklet and created an employee appraisal form that was tied to annual salary increases. She also made up salary guidelines that were approved by supervisors. Wendy wrote the museum's affirmative action plan and made sure that it was being followed. It was also her job to respond to discrimination issues. Wendy's responsibilities included serving as liaison between employees and management and managing the personnel procurement budget and the personal services budget for things that benefit employees in general.

Career Path. With a bachelor's degree in arts administration, Wendy had the academic background necessary for obtaining an administrative job at a museum. But she also had an additional strength—business experience from being the co-owner of a health food distribution company. Wendy answered a newspaper ad for a secretary at the Walker. Her prospective boss also wanted someone who could handle the human resources part of his job and thought she would be able to do this. Within one year, she was an administrative assistant, and three years later she was the human resources manager. Wendy's career path shows how a fulfilling career in an art museum can develop from an entry-level position.

Job Opportunities in Human Resources. The opportunity to obtain a job as human resources manager in an art museum is limited because only museums with fifty or more employees need a full-time staff member in this position. Quite often, this position is coupled with that of administrative director. According to the Association of Art Museum Directors, human resources managers at large museums earn a mean salary of $102,502 while the mean salary of those at smaller museums is $48,500.

A New Museum Job—Director of Information Technology

The computer age has brought the computer into every art museum where it is assigned so many tasks. It is now handling inventory, accounting, membership, ticketing, gift shop transactions, and building maintenance. Plus, museums now have websites that provide visitors an online look at selected items in the collection. E-mails are also being sent to patrons and visitors who may wish to see a particular exhibition. Because of the important role that computers have assumed in the operation of museums, art lovers who have computer expertise can now find jobs at museums.

For most of his career, Jim Horio has been involved in working with computers. His jobs have ranged from being employed at a cruise line to a bio-technology firm. At the same time, Jim is a culture lover who enjoys opera and ballet and has visited great museums around the world. His present job has given him the chance to work at the new Asian Art Museum of San Francisco—one of the finest collections of Asian art in the world—as director of information technology. While this is definitely a computer job, it is also perfect for a culture lover as Jim has the chance to work with art in so many ways. It has been especially meaningful as he has had the opportunity to design the entire computer system, which also includes kiosks through the museum to help visitors learn more about the collection. Each workday is a pleasure for Jim as he can always take a moment to study individual pieces in the collection. Art lovers definitely need to think beyond the box when they seek ways to combine vocation and avocation.

Art Galleries

Art lovers can purchase sculpture, etchings, antique prints, original fine art, tribal art, serigraphs, and limited-edition graphics at art galleries. They can also find jobs working in art galleries, for there are thousands of them in the United States. Furthermore, there is such a diversity in galleries that art lovers can look for a job in a gallery that sells the art of their favorite medium, style, period, or artists.

Art galleries can be as dissimilar as a small showroom in a tourist resort selling paintings and sculpture by local artists versus a ten-thousand-square-foot loft in a high-rent district in New York City selling paintings worth millions of dollars. Wherever art lovers choose to work, it is essential that they have a knowledge of art. At many galleries, this means having at least a bachelor's degree in art history, and for some galleries having a master's degree is required even for entry-level positions. In New York City, competition is so intense that job seekers try to get a foot in the door by working as interns for no wages or minimum wage or by taking the most lowly job available at a gallery.

Gallery Owner in a Midwestern City

Several years ago, Eckert Fine Art carried both antique furniture and nineteenth- and twentieth-century paintings, in addition to a few eighteenth-century pieces. As the owners of the gallery purchased exceptional estates that had paintings by renowned artists of the region, the gallery emerged as an art gallery that solely promoted the painting of regional artists, past and present. Today, the gallery, now called Eckert & Ross Fine Art, has tripled in size and also deals in nationally known American and European artists who paint in the traditional style.

From childhood, Jim Ross, a partner in the gallery, has had a keen interest in art and has always painted and sketched. Fortunately for this true aficionado of art, his jobs have always been associated with art in some way. While in college at the Herron School of Art, he worked at the Indianapolis Museum of Art in advertising and marketing. Then after graduating with a degree in visual communication, he continued to work at the museum until he left to form his own graphic design firm. Jim became acquainted with the owners of Eckert Fine Art through doing brochures for them. When the firm moved to more spacious quarters, he even helped the owners move. Shortly thereafter, he became assistant to the director of the gallery, then gallery director, and he is now a partner.

On the Job. Jim is able to spend his days working with art. He does not have to deal with administrative tasks, as they are handled by his partner. Jim spends most of his time selling art. This includes talking to clients in the gallery and on the phone. He acts as their consultant and guide in the purchase of paintings and even travels to their homes to hang paintings. Another aspect of his job is acquiring art for the gallery. Because there is a limited supply of art the gallery sells, part of his job is convincing people to sell their art. As the gallery has acquired a solid reputation for selling fine art, this task has become easier as more people wish to sell their art to the gallery.

Career Advice. Young art lovers should try to become familiar with those individuals who work with art. Knowing the owners of the gallery gave Jim the opportunity to demonstrate his expertise with art and work his way up to a partnership.

Gallery Owner in New York City

Major art galleries in New York City are extremely selective in choosing entry-level employees. Armed with a bachelor's degree in art history plus experience as a summer intern at the Metropolitan Museum of Art, Tim Nye went around to art galleries with his impressive resume looking for his first job. He found a job as a gallery assistant at Nancy Hoffman Gallery, where he handled art, made boxes for shipping, sent out packages, labeled slides, and went to clients' homes to hang art they had purchased. There was no glamour in this job, but it was a beginning. Tim's next job was as a cataloger at Robert Miller Gallery. A cataloging job involves taking photographs of art and writing the serial numbers on the back of the work. This was a particularly appropriate job, since Tim had written his thesis on one of the artists whose work was sold at this gallery.

Tim went away from the art world briefly to get an M.B.A. with a concentration in nonprofit organizations. He knew that he always wanted to return to the art world and did so during the summer after his first year of graduate school. With profits made from selling two paintings by a pop artist whose work swiftly escalated in price after the death of Andy Warhol, Tim was able to mount his own exhibition. He rented a temporary gallery space and put together a showing called "Three Painters." One of the painters was a friend, Paul Pagk, who had received recognition in France. After graduation from business school, Tim found a fabulous seventy-five-hundred-square-foot open loft. He was also able to obtain funding from a foundation for two one-person shows in his loft gallery. Each show was hung for about six weeks, longer than the typical one-month show in New York City. The success of previous shows allowed him to find funding for a third show, the works of a sculptor. Tim is trying to make his gallery a center for contemporary arts and is holding poetry readings and concerts in the gallery. In the future, Tim hopes to be selling art and continuing with his gallery.

More Careers for Art Lovers

Artists' Representatives

Both commercial and fine artists often need someone to bring them jobs. This is the role artists' representatives play: they sell artists' talents to people in a position to pay for the use of their talents. Shirley Talbert works full-time as a representative for commercial artists. Although she works in a firm that has another representative, most representatives work alone. To find companies that need commercial artists, she calls on art directors of advertising agencies, graphic designers, and corporations, talking to them about their needs. Her clientele is decidedly not a fixed group, and neither is the group of artists she represents, with new people always needing her services. Commercial artists call Shirley or send her resumes and portfolios of their work. She evaluates their artwork and tries to sign contracts for at least a year with the artists she decides to represent.

Much time and effort is required to market the work of an artist. Shirley works with the artist to create a portfolio that displays his or her distinctive style, which she can then show potential users of the artist's work. When a client requests an artist who can do a certain type of work, Shirley usually visits the client with the portfolios of three artists who have different styles. Her job as an artist representative does not end when an artist is selected by a client. She is responsible for seeing that the artist's work is completed on time and to the specifications of her client.

Shirley also works part-time on her own as a fine-artist representative. In this role, she finds a client first and then looks for an artist after spending considerable time consulting with the client on his or her needs. Being an artist's representative requires both business and art backgrounds, which Shirley has. Her business experience is derived from working in marketing after she graduated from college with a bachelor's degree in sales and marketing. Shirley acquired her knowledge of art through collecting paintings and graphics.

Art Advisors

Many people love art and would like to have excellent pieces of art in their homes. Communities often want to put on art exhibits for their residents. Corporations frequently want to have art collections. Government units often want paintings, sculptures, mosaics, and murals to decorate buildings. Because not everyone is an expert at selecting art, the career of art advisor has emerged. Art advisors are the experts who help people and organizations find the art they want. They do not deal in art or have an inventory of art. Their job is to be advisors. They can work alone or with a group.

Lynne Bear is an art advisor who works alone out of a home office. Most of her business is focused on helping organizations find art to be displayed in public places. She also advises individuals in the selection of art. In order to do this, she has a wide network of contacts in the art community that enables her to find the artwork that her clients want. She both buys art for clients and commissions artists to create pieces. In addition, she puts together works of art for exhibitions.

Career Path. Unlike many art lovers, Lynne was not always interested in art. It came to her as an adult when she visited museums for the very first time during a trip to Europe. On her return to the United States, Lynne set out to learn more about art, first by volunteering at museums and then by obtaining a master's degree in art history. Her first job in the art world was at a large regional auction house, where she started as the assistant director of painting with the responsibility of appraising art, finding works of art, and selling art. Before she left the firm to start her own business, she had become director of the fine arts department and had made excellent contacts within the art community.

Career Advice. Lynne advises people who want to have a job like hers to study the field of art history in an academic environment to gain a historic and aesthetic perspective as well as to get experience in a structured environment to gain the skills they will need. She believes that working in an auction house is an excellent way to learn a lot about art.

Art Appraisers

People often want to know the value of a work of art for buying or selling the piece or sometimes just to satisfy their curiosity. In addition, they may want information for insurance, tax, or estate purposes. The experts who decide the price or value of artwork are called appraisers. This career requires a thorough knowledge of art and a familiarity with the value of individual pieces of art.

Karen Tallackson was about eighteen when she decided that she wanted to be an art appraiser. To acquire the necessary background in art, she obtained both bachelor's and master's degrees in art history. She also studied art in England and France, where she had direct contact with many works of fine art. To begin to have an idea of the value of different pieces, she read a variety of art magazines. To gain more knowledge of art and valuing art, she started as an intern at a firm of international fine art auctioneers and appraisers; she later became an appraiser with this company.

Her internship project was to create a chronological dictionary of California paintings. This helped Karen become familiar with the artists and their styles, as well as with previous auction prices of their works. When her internship was completed, Karen became administrative assistant to the director. This allowed her to become familiar with the clientele of the auction house and auction procedures.

After Karen expressed an interest in contemporary art, the firm let her start making appraisals from photographs that were sent to the firm for evaluation. In her next position as inventory manager, she inventoried every piece of art that came into the firm by entering it into the computer. This meant she was actually seeing and handling works of art. According to Karen, the more art a prospective appraiser sees, the more skilled the individual becomes in making qualitative judgments. She also learned more about the art market by talking to clients.

Prospective appraisers can learn more about the job by contacting the American Society of Appraisers, which also has a student organization. The society provides accreditation to professional appraisers. For more information, contact:

American Society of Appraisers
555 Herndon Parkway, Suite 125
Herndon, VA 20170
www.appraisers.org

On the Way to Becoming an Appraiser. After the contemporary art appraiser left the fine arts firm, Karen became the company's contemporary art appraiser. One of her duties was to make insurance appraisals. She also found properties for the firm's semiannual contemporary art auctions. She acquired properties for these sales from all over the country, which meant spending considerable time on the phone. When a piece arrived at the firm, Karen had it photographed and entered information about it on the computer. For each auction, she created the catalog that described the artist, the work of art, and the pre-auction estimate. Appraisers must know the market, so Karen was always going to galleries and openings plus reading the *Journal of Art* and the *International Art Newsletter* to keep abreast of pricing and market trends. Karen left this job to work for a company establishing an online art gallery.

Being an appraiser is an opportunity for art lovers to have daily contact with art. Besides requiring an excellent knowledge of the media that the appraiser values, phone and computer skills are essential, as is an ability to deal with people.

Fine Art Auctioneers

At fine arts auctions, people bid for antiques, jewelry, and collectibles as well as fine art. To prepare for an auction, auctioneers must study the catalog for the auction and learn which items are most important. They also talk with department people about the items to be auctioned.

You do not go to school to become an auctioneer. Instead, you learn by watching other auctioneers and then developing your own style. A very important characteristic for auctioneers is self-confidence. To become a successful fine arts auctioneer, it is necessary to have an in-depth knowledge of the art that you are auctioning.

Art Critics

According to David Bonetti, art critic for the *St. Louis Post-Dispatch*, art critics can be divided into two groups. In one group, you will find the critics who write for art journals. Their audience is assumed to be knowledgeable about art, so specialized vocabulary can be used in these critics' pieces. In the other group are the critics who write for daily or weekly newspapers with large circulations. They cannot assume that their readers have any more than a basic knowledge of art, so they write in a straightforward way, reporting on art-related events. Some newspaper art critics just report the facts. Others, like David, write more about what artists are trying to do and whether they are successful in achieving their own goals. He also feels it is important to explain to his readers what the newest art is all about.

Unlike music and theater critics on newspaper staffs, art critics seldom have an overnight deadline. It is not as important for them to report immediately on the opening of a new show at a gallery or museum because, in most cases, people will have many opportunities to see the show. Not having the pressure of a deadline gives the art critic time to reflect on a new show.

This job should be very appealing to art lovers because you are able to spend considerable time looking at art in museums, galleries, and other exhibit venues. The job also involves a great deal of reading about art. For example, David had to study a four-hundred-page catalog to learn about the background, history, aesthetics, and cultural context of an exhibit of Indonesian art at a museum. With contemporary art, there is rarely a catalog, so he has to do some background research, which may itself become part of a future catalog.

Unfortunately, there are not a great number of jobs for art critics at newspapers, since only major newspapers employ full-time critics. In addition, the outlook for more newspaper jobs for art critics is not rosy. The number of newspapers in the United States is steadily dropping, with approximately one thousand fewer newspapers today than in the early 1900s. Furthermore, many major newspapers are losing circulation to suburban papers.

Career Path. There is no one route to becoming an art critic at a newspaper. The precise job requirements are not something that can be studied at school. Obviously, an ability to write and a knowledge of art are basic requirements. Many art critics, according to David, started out wanting to be artists or writers—especially poets—and then redirected their interests to critical writing. However, David's path to becoming an art critic followed a different route. After majoring in literature and taking many art courses in college, he taught preschool—specializing in art and literature.

From teaching he went to work in sales at an art gallery. While working in the gallery, he started writing art reviews for a monthly publication. He heard of an opening at a Boston paper for an art critic, sent them his clippings, and got the job. His next career move was to the San Francisco *Examiner*. When this paper merged with the much larger *San Francisco Chronicle*, David worked there for a year before moving to his current position at the *St. Louis Post-Dispatch*. "Being an art critic," David says, "is being paid to work with my interest." It is decidedly not a nine-to-five job for him. Even on off days he is at galleries and museums pursuing his interest in art.

Art Teachers

While a very limited number of art students ultimately become professional artists, most gain an appreciation of art through their classes in school. Art lovers who wish to share their love of art with others will find teaching art a rewarding career. Teaching lets practicing art lovers introduce future art lovers to different media and the history of art and artists through the ages.

Qualifications. Individuals wishing to teach art in public schools need to earn bachelor's degrees in education with training in art education. Most also obtain their master's degrees early in their teaching careers. At the college or university level, having a doctorate or master of fine arts degree (the most advanced degree in the studio arts) is a prerequisite for all art teachers, with the occasional exception of those who have attained acclaim as outstanding artists.

Demand. Art lovers wishing to teach in elementary school will find that the current demand for art teachers is reduced in many areas because of budget cutting. At the high school level, fewer art teachers are needed in many states because, in addition to budget cuts, more required courses have been added to the curriculum, which means fewer students can choose art classes as electives. In colleges and universities, competition for positions teaching art is as intense as it is in all other areas of instruction.

Salaries. While the average salary for all public school teachers is currently about $45,000 a year, beginning teachers earn an average salary of about $30,000. With each year of experience, teachers' salaries climb according to the salary scale of the school district. Salaries also increase as teachers gain additional degrees or college units. Teachers in private schools generally earn less than those who teach in public schools. Overall, teacher salaries range from about $25,000 to close to $70,000. At the college and university level, average salaries are between $25,000 and $63,000.

Art from the Cart

Sonia Fernandez is an elementary school art teacher. She has taught in beautiful, fully equipped art rooms, in cafeterias, and in science rooms; she has also pushed a cart loaded with art supplies from room to room. Teaching art can be a hectic experience in an elementary school. Art teachers never seem to have enough time to get everything done. Supplies have to be taken out and put back for each class, and a project must be completed in thirty or forty-five minutes.

According to Sonia, an hour would be an ideal amount of time for an art class, especially for students in the intermediate grades, but this rarely happens. Art lovers planning to teach art should also realize that they may see every student in the school during the course of the week. This often means teaching art to more than five hundred students.

Art teachers also have demands made on their time to prepare such things as posters for paper drives and props or scenery for a school musical or play, plus help children participate in art competitions. Add in the frustration of crowded classrooms, and you might wonder why Sonia enjoys teaching art and would not think of teaching any other class. The reason is simple: she thoroughly enjoys introducing young children to the world of art.

A Lifetime of Teaching Art

Jim Doversberger always knew he wanted to be an art teacher, and that is the one and only job he has ever had, except for a short stint in the navy. Jim brought a solid knowledge of art to his teaching career, since he earned both bachelor's and master's degrees in fine arts. He took education courses and did student teaching to qualify for his teaching credential. While attending Herron Art School, he taught art classes every Saturday morning. He continued teaching these classes for many years after he became a full-time teacher because he liked teaching classes to children of different ages.

Jim first learned of his future teaching job from a notice on the bulletin board at the art school. Prospective art teachers can still learn about positions in this way, as well as through college placement offices, newspapers, professional organizations, and the Internet. Jim applied for the job and was hired as an art teacher. When he first started at Lawrence Central High School, he was the only art teacher at this small suburban high school. Over the course of his career, the suburb grew and the art faculty expanded until there were six art teachers, and Jim was department chair. The number of art teachers was reduced when another high school was built in the district and further reduced to one full-time position and one part-time position when fewer students began to take art because of increased requirements in science and social studies.

A typical course load for Jim would be teaching beginning art, drawing, and graphics; intermediate drawing and painting; and advanced art. His classes averaged twenty-six students at the beginning level, but as few as twelve at the advanced level. On the intermediate level, Jim always devoted Friday to teaching art history. He and the other art teachers in the district had the opportunity to develop their own curricula within the broad guidelines of the state requirements. Most experienced teachers are able to develop their own curricula in this way.

Art teachers, like other teachers, have responsibilities that extend beyond the classroom. Jim sponsored an art club at times throughout his career; in the early part of his career, before a stagecraft teacher was hired, he designed the stage sets for the school's two annual productions. When an empty room turned up at the school, he established an art gallery that featured revolving shows of the students' artwork. Much time every year was devoted to helping students prepare for major art competitions. He served on the board of the regional scholastic art competition, and some of his time was spent judging other competitions.

Jim spent considerable time painting at the start of his teaching career. Then this lover of the arts switched his interest to the local theater and appeared in more than sixty-five plays. Teaching does give art lovers time to pursue their interests in the summer. Jim frequently traveled to Europe to visit art museums. He also attended workshops during the summer.

Additional Career Options

Wherever a collection of art is located, there exist possible jobs for art lovers. Art lovers should investigate the possibilities of working at corporations because, like museums and art galleries, they may have art collections that require curators, conservators, art historians, and librarians. For example, Bank of America and Goldman Sachs & Company have sizeable art collections that are predominantly displayed in the firms' hallways and offices. Curators of collections in the corporate world, besides loaning pieces to employees for their offices, often launch programs to educate employees about art.

Today's libraries also offer job opportunities for art lovers. Many libraries have programs that involve the loaning of works of art. In addition, librarians with a knowledge of art are needed in the art departments of major libraries.

Beyond the world of fine art, there is the rather large world of commercial art. You can imagine the size of this world when you think of all the advertisements that bombard you from billboards, newspapers, magazines, catalogs, and radio and television stations. In each of these arenas, there are scores of employees dealing with the development of commercial art designed to sell products to the public. Many jobs, especially in advertising agencies and commercial art studios, involve working directly with art.

Whenever art lovers see art that appeals to them, they are also seeing job opportunities in buying, selling, displaying, and choosing this art. Being involved in art is not just a job for its creators.

CHAPTER THREE

Career Opportunities for Music Lovers

Working with Symphonies, Operas, and Other Forms of Music

Music must take rank as the highest of the fine arts—as the one which, more than any other, ministers to the human spirit.
—Herbert Spencer

J ust look around at people in shopping malls, on airplanes, and on jogging paths—so many of them are moving to the music playing on their Walkmans or iPods. Music lovers have the unique advantage of being able to enjoy music in a great variety of everyday settings. And the range of music that they can enjoy is enormous, from pop tunes to classical symphonies. If music lovers want to extend their interest in music beyond a beloved avocation, there are many careers that allow them to be associated with music in some way.

In recent years, music has turned into a multibillion dollar business offering careers to thousands of people. There are opportunities to work with a symphony, opera, or ballet company; in radio and television; in the recording and record business; with music retailers and wholesalers; in education; and in the crafting, repair, and restoration of musical instruments. Wherever music is played, created, sold, or enjoyed, music lovers should investigate career opportunities. You do not need to be a trained musician to have a job in the music world. Many jobs exist on the business side for staff publicists, promotion managers, music shop salespersons, personal managers, booking agents, and business managers. Just a glance at the music section in the yellow pages of your local telephone directory will give you an idea of the number of companies in your community that are connected with music.

While music is a performing art, few individuals are able to support themselves as full-time performers. Many musicians elect to combine performing with jobs that allow them to be closely associated with music in the workplace. They can be employed as music teachers, music therapists, copyists, recording engineers, instrument restorers, disc jockeys, librarians, choir directors, arrangers, and in an amazing variety of other jobs closely associated with music.

Today, as in the past, music plays a key role in culture. Six thousand years ago in Egypt, court musicians were playing harps and wind and percussion instruments while military bands used trumpets and drums. In our modern world, music continues to play an important role in ceremonial occasions, from White House receptions to parades. It also occupies a significant place in such disparate activities as preschoolers singing "Twinkle, Twinkle, Little Star" to teenagers creating rap songs to adults enjoying symphonies and operas.

Teaching Music

Teaching music is an excellent way to share a love of music with others—from fledgling musicians in preschool to skilled graduate students in a university. Since each age level offers different challenges and rewards, prospective music teachers will need to decide which age group is most appealing to them. At all levels, music teachers in schools have a number of duties that must be performed, from taking attendance to giving grades. In addition, there are frequently state, local, or school guidelines that prescribe the curriculum that is to be taught in music classes. Besides normal teaching duties, most music teachers will usually spend time before and after school working with different musical groups or preparing students for special contests and performances.

The Music Educators National Conference (MENC) website includes an online page titled "Why Teach, Why Music, Why Me?" It provides information about jobs and preparing for jobs in music education. To learn more about careers in teaching music, contact:

Music Educators National Conference (MENC)
1806 Robert Fulton Drive
Reston, VA 20191
www.menc.org

You can also learn more about the profession by studying professional journals, such as these publications, which can be found in university libraries and some public libraries:

American Music Teacher (www.mtna.org/amt.htm)
American String Teacher (www.astaweb.com/journal.htm)
The Choral Journal (www.acdaonline.org/cj)
Contributions to Music Education (www.cme.webhop.org)

Besides information on teaching, a few of these journals offer some job listings for music teachers. Libraries also have state publications concerned with music education that frequently post advertisements for teaching positions.

Job Qualifications and Opportunities

Elementary and secondary school music teachers normally hold bachelor's degrees with majors in music education. During the course of their teaching careers, many will also obtain master's degrees. Current funding difficulties in the public schools, coupled with the fact that music is not considered a basic subject, have led to a tighter job market for prospective music teachers. Individuals seeking employment as music teachers usually learn of job opportunities through college placement bureaus, employment fairs, newspaper advertisements, networking with other teachers, and the Internet. Many also contact school districts to see if there are positions available for music teachers.

College and university music teachers who teach theory classes are usually required to have a doctorate in some aspect of music; however, exceptions are made for those who teach performance classes if they have the press clippings to demonstrate a national reputation in their teaching areas. Competition is extremely intense for positions at this level, and many qualified people are competing for few jobs.

Salaries

The average salary of music teachers in public elementary and secondary schools is the same as that of all other teachers. Experienced teachers may earn as much as $70,000, while beginning teachers may start with salaries in the mid-$20,000 range. Overall, the average salary for teachers is about $45,000 a year. At the college level, salaries range from $18,000 to $150,000 a year, depending on faculty rank, experience, degrees earned, and the size, location, and status of the institution.

Teaching in an Elementary School

Julia Scherer has taught music at the same elementary school for more than twenty years. She plans to stay at this school until she takes early retirement to publish the school musicals she has written and to make commercials. Not able to find a job as a music teacher after graduation from college with a bachelor's degree in music education, Julia applied for a job as a substitute teacher—only to find that the district was looking for a music teacher. She applied for the job, was hired, and is still working at this school.

Like most music teachers, Julia has obtained a master's degree in music and has taken other additional courses to keep her teaching credential up-to-date.

As an elementary music specialist, Julia teaches general music classes that feature instruction in vocal music, composition, reading music, instruments of the orchestra, music appreciation, and playing the recorder—depending on the grade levels of her students. In addition to her hours at school, she spends time planning and presenting three major musicals, two spring sings, and choir and recorder ensemble programs each year. Twice a week, she comes in early to give special instruction to the ensemble groups. Most elementary school music teachers have similar responsibilities.

Inspired by her elementary and high school music teachers to choose a career teaching music, Julia transmits her love of music to her students. In turn, she was introduced by one of her former students, who had a major role in the musical *Cats*, to the cast backstage as the lady who got him started in music. Knowing her students appreciate her efforts is what makes her career so satisfying.

Like most music teachers, Julia finds that her involvement with music does not end in the classroom. Over the years, she has directed children's church choirs, given private voice lessons, sung with an entertainment company, and starred in numerous community theater productions, receiving many awards for her singing and acting ability in these shows.

Teaching in a Junior High School

It is a challenging job to create an orchestra, choir, or band from a group of students in sixth, seventh, and eighth grades. Many of these students have never sung a note or held a musical instrument in their hands before the first day in the music classroom. This is a challenge that faces junior high school music teachers like Joe Zaharako every day.

Joe is the band director at a large junior high school. His teaching responsibilities include teaching band to students in sixth, seventh, and eighth grades, along with a general music class for sixth graders. Other teachers at this school concentrate on teaching choir or orchestra, along with a few classes in general music. At smaller schools, music teachers should expect to teach both vocal and instrumental music classes. One of the most appealing aspects of Joe's job is seeing how his students develop as musicians during the three years they spend at the school.

Joe's educational background includes a bachelor's degree and a master's degree in music education, the typical education pattern for music teachers. His time spent with music is not limited to teaching; he is also a member of a brass choir.

Teaching in a High School

Thomas Dick was not born into a musically inclined family; his father did not even recognize a cello when his son brought one home. However, from an early age music just seemed like the natural thing for Thomas to do. He became a very skilled cellist, playing first chair in several community orchestras. During college, he made the decision to become a teacher rather than a performer because he wanted to help young people. He was able to pay for his education with a music scholarship plus jobs as a cellist with a symphony orchestra and as a string bass player in a group that performed at supper clubs. Thomas also played in the orchestra for road shows like *Fiddler on the Roof* and *The Sound of Music*. A great number of music teachers earn part of their college tuition by working as performers.

Since completing his bachelor's degree in music education, Thomas has taught at three high schools, obtaining his master's degree in music education along the way. In his present job, he is the director of orchestras at a large suburban high school. He teaches four periods of strings and one period of wind and percussion each day. During a typical strings class, he begins by having the students play scales for intonation, quality of sound, and technique. Most of the period is devoted to working on problems with current pieces, with some time devoted to sight reading and the teaching of musical terms, abbreviations, and signs.

The days are long for a high school music teacher. Four days a week, Thomas supervises rehearsals of different sections of the orchestra after school; every Tuesday evening he holds a three-hour rehearsal of performance and possible contest pieces to discover problems that the students can work on at home and in their sections. Thomas receives a stipend for the work he does with students beyond the regular school day, as most high school music teachers do.

During the school year, he is the guest conductor for junior and senior high school orchestras and acts as a judge at several music contests. He also finds time to serve on the board of the state school music association. In the summer, Thomas often acts as the orchestra director of a summer music camp. Today, when this busy music teacher has time, he sings in a church choir. During his teaching career, he has also at various times directed choirs and played the cello with different symphony groups.

Thomas's goal is to give his students a good experience in his orchestra classes, which he hopes will lead to a lifetime of enjoying good music and the playing of a musical instrument. He sees himself as being a student-oriented music teacher rather than a performance-oriented teacher. Because he is so sensitive to the needs of his students, the walls of his office abound with plaques and letters of appreciation, like the one he received from his orchestra students when he left the school for his present position:

A Tribute to the Conductor. As our teacher, we have both loved and admired him, for he has been much more than a simple instructor. Not only has he been the key to our musical growth, but he has been our friend and our inspiration as well. Through him we have been encouraged to better ourselves both with music and in our daily lives.

As our conductor, he has shared with us his wonderful gift of music. Through his help and guidance we have each been allowed to develop our inner talents into a product that we can use to bring joy to others.

Teaching in a College

Martin Marks dreamed of being a performer as a child—a dream he realized by playing the piano with symphony orchestras and giving solo recitals in the Midwest. Besides performing, he also gave piano lessons to as many as one hundred students a week and studied for his bachelor's and master's degrees in music with a performance orientation. His outstanding reputation as a teacher and pianist led to his appointment as a part-time and then a full-time professor of music. Today, he gives classes in piano literature and overcoming performance anxiety and teaches piano to college students and a few private students.

Private Music Instruction

Being a private music teacher is an excellent way to combine teaching and a love of music. Working in their own homes, in students' homes, and in studios, these teachers usually instruct school-aged children. The number of students depends on the local demand as well as the individual's reputation as a skilled teacher. Since most of their students are in school during the day, a private teacher's day does not normally begin until school is over.

Fees. Fees range from $10 to $100 per lesson, although some experts command much higher fees. What you earn depends greatly on your reputation as well as the demand for music instruction in your area.

A Private Teacher

With an educational background of a bachelor's degree in music education, a minor in music therapy, and a master's in performance, Melissa Williams has taught music in elementary school and worked at a residential treatment center for emotionally disturbed children. Today, she teaches tuba, euphonium, and trombone to about forty students, plays in symphony orchestras in two cities, and does some freelancing at recording studios.

To get started as a private teacher in a new city, she joined a brass choir and played with a local symphony, where she met many school music teachers who have recommended her to students in their classes. In her free time Melissa practices the tuba, hoping to win an audition to be a regular in a major symphony orchestra. To hone her skills, this accomplished musician takes lessons from an expert player with the Chicago Symphony.

Music Therapists—Helping People Through Music

Music therapists are a bold, aggressive group of professionals who are pounding on the doors of hospitals and other treatment centers, explaining how adding a music therapist would enhance the facility. Although people have been helped by music through the ages, it is only since the 1950s that music therapists have been slowly accepted by the medical profession as a part of its treatment team. The American Music Therapy Association describes music therapy as the use of music in the accomplishment of therapeutic aims: the restoration, maintenance, and improvement of mental and physical health.

As a result of their efforts, music therapists are now being added to the staffs at some hospices, nursing homes, rehabilitation centers, prisons, school systems, clinics, and day care and treatment centers for children. At the same time, due to current budget restraints, many music therapists are being forced to take jobs with titles such as activity director or program director—which means that music is only a small part of their jobs.

Music therapists do not just work in institutions. Freelance music therapists continue working with patients who have been discharged from a hospital, easing the adjustment back into the community. Therapists also work in their studios with young children and adults who have been referred to them by health professionals.

As members of a treatment team, music therapists work with doctors, social workers, occupational therapists, nurses, and psychologists. As individuals, the team members meet with new patients and assess how their disciplines can help these people. Then the team meets and discusses the role each discipline will play in helping in the patient's recovery and sets goals for the treatment plan. The committee meets again every few months to review each patient's progress.

The music therapist uses music and music activities, usually in a group setting, to bring about desirable changes in behavior. Since music has a great effect on people's feelings and emotions, it helps the patients share their thoughts with others in a nonthreatening manner.

Qualifications

Music therapists need to be emotionally stable individuals who can work well with both their clients and the personnel of the therapeutic treatment team. They also find it helpful to be able to play more than one musical instrument. Becoming a music therapist requires a bachelor's degree in music therapy with courses in music, music therapy, psychology, and the social sciences, followed by an internship at an approved treatment facility.

After completing the degree program or equivalent and an internship, a music therapist can acquire the credential Music Therapist–Board Certified (MT–BC) by passing the national examination administered by the independent Certification Board for Music Therapists. This ensures that a music therapist has the highest professional qualifications. For more information, contact:

Certification Board for Music Therapists
506 East Lancaster Avenue, Suite 102
Downingtown, PA 19335
www.cbmt.org

Salaries

The salary range for music therapists is from less than $20,000 to more than $70,000 a year. According to the National Association for Music Education, the approximate salary range for music therapists working in the following areas is as follows:

Hospitals and Psychiatric Facilities	$20,000–$60,000
Special Education Facility	$22,000–$42,000
Clinic for Disabled Children	$15,000–$70,000
Mental Health Center	$21,000–$65,000
Nursing Home	$17,000–$65,000
Correctional Facility	$23,000–$58,000
Private Practice	$18,000–$77,000

Benefits vary greatly depending on the facility where a therapist works. Many jobs in state and federal facilities offer the benefits of civil service positions.

For More Information

The American Music Therapy Association has more information on becoming a music therapist, including a list of the colleges and universities that offer degree programs in the field. For more information, contact:

American Music Therapy Association
8455 Colesville Road, Suite 1000
Silver Spring, MD 20910
www.musictherapy.org

A Music Therapist's Job

After learning more about music therapy, Barbara Romerhaus switched her major from music education to music therapy because she enjoyed helping people and liked working in hospital treatment facilities. She concentrated on piano and flute in college, but then learned to play the Autoharp and different percussion, string, and woodwind instruments in order to be able to help future patients using a variety of instruments.

Barbara's first job was as acting director of music therapy at a state hospital. She could not be appointed director because the facility required two years of experience for appointment to this position. Barbara worked a forty-hour week setting up patient choir groups, teaching musical skills groups, and helping patients tap into community resources when they left the hospital. It is an important part of the job for music therapists to find community music groups where discharged patients can go to continue their music interests.

Barbara's next job was on a research project in a psychiatric hospital, doing a study of autistic children under the direction of a major university. Like all research studies, the program was very structured. Barbara worked with ten autistic children, teaching them various motor skills, concepts like "up and down" and "right and left," and even numbers and letters through music and song. According to Barbara, music helps people learn and remember information better than any other medium because of the structure within it. Music is also used as positive reinforcement toward attaining the desired behavior change. The children responded positively to the music and were rewarded by being able to listen to favorite songs. Some of the children had language skills, while others let Barbara know their musical preferences through body language.

After two years with the research program, Barbara became the director of the hospital's adult music therapy program. Her duties were quite similar to those of her first job at the state hospital. She conducted classes in such areas as music and relaxation, music and movement to help increase the patients' energy and motivation, and music and recreation to help patients acquire leisure skills.

After an eleven-year break in her career path to raise a family, Barbara returned to music therapy at a state hospital—illustrating that a career in this profession can be resumed after even a break of more than a decade. She became the rehabilitation therapy supervisor at the hospital with twelve people under her supervision, including two music therapists, two occupational therapists, a recreational therapist, and therapy assistants. Her duties included administering, planning, and making sure that the programs her staff members were conducting met the needs of the patients. She also had to make sure her staff worked within the allotted budget, and she attended hospital administrators' meetings. In addition, she was in charge of the music therapy internship program at her facility.

Music Librarians

Libraries with large collections of music books, recordings, musical scores, and periodicals associated with music have jobs for music librarians. The focus of music collections in public libraries is usually general, with materials ranging from popular to classical music. Some libraries, like the Library of Congress and the New York Public Library, have so much information about music that they serve as research centers. Academic libraries have more scholarly materials than most public libraries, and some specialize in a particular area, such as the jazz library at Rutgers University. Music librarians can also find jobs at places that have large music collections that need to be kept in order, such as radio and television stations, large music publishers, and professional music associations.

Most music libraries are quite small and specialized, so music librarians typically have to perform a variety of tasks, from dealing with patrons to handling administrative duties. Library patrons can add great interest to this job as you may work with young music students, music teachers, professional artists, and researchers. In this job, you are most likely to work at a large university or in a large city. Because the field is so small, there is limited opportunity for advancement.

It is not easy to become a music librarian. Most music librarians have master's degrees in library science from an accredited program of the American Library Association. For many positions, they are also required to have master's or even doctoral degrees in some aspect of music.

Nevertheless, music lovers do not need advanced degrees to work in music libraries, as there are jobs there for clerks who usually have completed technical or associate degrees in library science. Almost everyone working in music libraries works with library clients, so skill in interacting with people is another job requirement.

Salaries

Annual salaries for music librarians who work in college, university, public, or orchestra libraries range between $18,000 and $45,000, according to the National Association for Music Education. Music librarians who work in special libraries earn slightly more. Library technicians have salaries between $14,000 and $38,000.

A Music Librarian

Equipped with a bachelor's degree in music education, Anna Thompson spent three years teaching music before returning to college to earn a master's degree in library science. She obtained her job as a music librarian in a major Midwest city through an interview held at her college. Because the music library was large, the music librarians specialized. Anna was in charge of all the sound recordings and cassette tapes, and she made selections of scores to be added to the band and ensemble sections. Part of her duties consisted of developing educational programs for the general public and the schools. For example, she organized a series of woodwind recitals, which required her to compile a bibliography, select performers, finalize contracts with them, and handle the publicity for the event.

Most professions have associations that allow members to extend their knowledge of the profession and to network with others in the field. Anna found further satisfaction in her career by being very active in the Music Library Association. She chaired the public library committee and served as chair for local arrangements when the association met in her city. To find out more about being a music librarian, contact:

Music Library Association
8551 Research Way, Suite 180
Middleton, WI 53562
www.musiclibraryassoc.org

Symphony Orchestras

When the conductors of the more than fifteen hundred symphony orchestras in the United States raise their batons to begin a performance, there are always people behind the scenes seeing to the orchestra's management. The larger a symphony is, the greater the number of people required to handle such administrative tasks as raising funds, marketing, publicizing the group, negotiating contracts, and handling the finances.

Although jobs with these orchestras are very appealing to music lovers, the number of jobs is definitely limited: there are only thirty major symphony orchestras in the United States. Job titles and responsibilities vary depending on the orchestra; however, music lovers are likely to find the following or similar administrative positions with major orchestras in these areas:

- **Managing Director:** responsible for all aspects of operating an orchestra and must implement policies of the symphony board.
- **Operations Manager:** assists the managing director in the operation of the orchestra.
- **Director of Development:** responsible for all fund-raising programs.
- **Business Manager:** handles all financial matters.
- **Publicity Director:** deals with the press and manages all aspects of promoting an orchestra.
- **Director of Education:** works with schools in developing concerts and other educational activities.
- **Ticket Service Director:** in charge of the sale of tickets.

Besides these top management positions, music lovers can find at least seventy more jobs at major orchestras as part of the administrative staff. These jobs include such positions as:

administrative assistant
payroll and benefits administrator
artistic coordinator
production coordinator
operations manager
controller
orchestra personnel manager
house manager
maintenance worker
building engineer
program manager
ticketing services
donor relations associate
gift processing coordinator
customer service representative
information services manager

Fewer jobs are available at medium-sized orchestras, while smaller orchestras may employ only a manager who is assisted by volunteers. Community orchestras may just employ a part-time manager or be completely run by volunteers.

Symphony orchestras hiring administrative staff look for individuals who have a background in music coupled with bachelor's or master's degrees in business or arts administration. Music lovers who want to work in this area will find it easier to get jobs if they have worked with a symphony as a volunteer or intern.

Symphony Career Information

If you are considering a career on the administrative side, a wealth of information exists for you through the American Symphony Orchestra League. The League's website lists names and information about most of the symphony orchestras in the United States. You should also investigate the Orchestra Management Fellowship Program, which provides year-long leadership training designed to launch executive careers in orchestra management through the observation of management practices in host orchestras, an intense course of study, and valuable hands-on work experiences. Fellowship program graduates hold more than seventy-eight leadership positions in American orchestras. Music lovers will learn more helpful information about the program by reading the blogs on the website of program participants. For more information, contact:

American Symphony Orchestra League
33 West Sixtieth Street
New York, NY 10023
www.symphony.org

Working as Director of Development

Raising money is never an easy job, but that is the number one responsibility of directors of development for symphony orchestras. They plan, coordinate, and implement all fund-raising programs. Sponsoring cocktail parties, gala dinners, symphony balls, and other special events are some of the ways that directors of development raise funds. They may also initiate direct mail campaigns and telethons as money raisers.

Time must also be spent searching and applying for business and government grants. Since volunteers play such an important role in soliciting funds, development directors must devise programs to recognize their invaluable help. Part of the director's job is to approve all newsletters, news releases, and fund-raising literature. And the director must also supervise staff and run the department within the budget.

The secret to success in this position is in producing results—successfully raising money. You will need to be an enthusiastic and persuasive individual to bring in donors. In order to advance, many directors move to larger and more prestigious symphony orchestras.

Salaries. What you earn as a director depends on the size of the orchestra. A small orchestra may only offer $12,000 a year, while larger orchestras pay $60,000 and up per year.

Assistant Vice President for Development and Marketing

The Indianapolis Symphony Orchestra (ISO) is one the nation's few full-time, fifty-two-week-season orchestras. As assistant vice president for development and marketing, Bob Swaney has responsibilities in the areas of earned income, patron services, endowment, planned giving, and major gifts. Due to the goals for growth that are budgeted in ticket sales, he currently is focusing on the marketing part of his job title, but he maintains some fund-raising responsibilities. However, on a typical fund-raising day, he may spend time with board-level volunteers who help in fund-raising, perform data analysis to make adjustments to gift-giving programs, ask potential and past donors for contributions to the orchestra, and connect symphony sponsors with events. This is not an eight-hour day job. In the evening, Bob often attends the symphony, where he entertains people at concerts and visits the founders' room to touch base with the patrons of the orchestra. Bob thinks that he has a wonderful job, as he has always been passionate about music and even has a degree in music, though he has never wished to be a performer.

Career Path. Bob started working with a symphony orchestra when he was still in college. Part-time jobs in an area that appeals to music lovers are a great way for job seekers to discover whether such a career is right for them and also get a foot in the door toward future employment. While still in college, Bob started out in telemarketing, making calls to prospective donors for a small symphony. After graduation, with this experience under his belt, he progressed to managing the telephone sales efforts of the Indianapolis Symphony. Then he branched into working with corporate donors and the annual fund.

A move to the Chicago Symphony, where he worked with the annual fund and government grants and was the director of development of the training orchestra, solidified for Bob that a career in development was right for him. He then worked as the development director for the St. Louis Symphony Orchestra before taking his current position in Indianapolis. Bob points out that people in his field must be willing to be mobile in order to advance.

Entry-Level Positions in Development

Large symphony orchestras frequently have internship and summer positions that give a bird's-eye view of what working in development is like. These positions usually involve working on small projects, and they help individuals gain valuable work experience. Before applying for an entry-level position in development, you should have a college degree and some fund-raising experience. A few schools have degrees in arts administration or management, which is the preferred degree for this job. If this is not possible, applicants should have taken course work in marketing, public relations, and business.

On the job, entry-level workers in development are typically assigned tasks associated with donors. They plan events for donors and accommodate their needs for tickets. If their work is effective, they will be on the path to upward mobility in this career.

Corporate Relations Associate

Emily Meaux is a music lover. She studied piano for ten years and was very involved with her high school choral program. In college, Emily majored in psychology and also obtained the American Humanics Certificate in Nonprofit Management and Leadership. Her first job opportunity in development occurred through networking. A speaker came to one of Emily's classes and spoke about careers with nonprofit organizations. When he heard that she was moving to Indianapolis, he told Emily that he could put her into contact with someone at the Indianapolis Symphony Orchestra. Emily sent her resume to this person, who gave it to the individual who was hiring. An interview soon lead to a job as a corporate relations associate after graduation.

At first, Emily worked three days a week and attended school for two days as she studied for a master's degree in nonprofit management. Her job was primarily administrative and involved writing proposals, tracking donations, and doing mailings. After a year, Emily became a full-time worker. She kept the same job title, but she had added responsibilities. It became her job to see that corporate donors received the benefits they were entitled to for sponsoring the symphony. This is a job of immense variety as no two sponsors have exactly the same benefits, and each sponsor has twenty-five to thirty benefits. For example, a car dealership may want a car displayed on the night it sponsors the symphony. In this case, Emily may actually drive the car from the dealership to the concert hall and ensure that it is displayed in a prominent location. She also makes sure that the sponsors' names appear in the program book and on sponsorship signs in the lobby and that they receive complimentary tickets. Daily tasks can range from having chocolates stamped with a sponsor's name for the company's guests to coordinating a post-concert party for fifteen hundred people. While Emily is working full-time, she also continues to take courses toward her master's degree.

Career Path. Emily is convinced that this is the right career sector for her. It is also an added dividend for this music lover that she is working for a symphony orchestra. After Emily obtains her graduate degree, she hopes to move up the career ladder locally or with another nonprofit organization.

Publicity Director

While the musicians are busy playing and the director of development is trying to raise funds, the publicity director is telling the media about the orchestra and promoting future symphony performances. Newspapers, magazines, radio stations, and television stations have to be notified about special events such as children's concerts and holiday programs. Stories must be followed so that the publicity director or one of the staff members can determine whether additional interviews or photos are needed.

Salaries. The size of the orchestra influences how much a public relations specialist earns. According to the National Association for Music Education, the salaries of those working in music communications start at about $21,000 a year.

A Media Relations Manager

At the Indianapolis Symphony Orchestra, the position of publicity director is called media relations manager. For the past fifteen years, this job has been held by Tim Northcutt. He is a music lover—an absolute requirement for this position. Tim can still recall the incredible experience that he had attending his first lollipop concert (a symphony program for children). His love of music continued in college, where his roommates were music majors and he became hooked on opera.

Courses in journalism and political science helped Tim obtain his first job in public relations, working as media secretary for a congressional candidate during his senior year in college. Successful work on this campaign led to stints as a reporter covering the Indiana General Assembly and campaign jobs for governors, senators, mayors, and congressional representatives in Kansas, California, Texas, Minnesota, Arizona, and Florida.

Desiring to stay in one place after marriage, Tim accepted a job at the Tampa Bay Performing Arts Center, a huge $57 million complex that holds more than eight hundred performances a year within its three theaters. At the center, Tim dealt with all kinds of entertainers, from comedians to opera stars. The center wanted Tim for this position because of his media background in dealing with *Time*, *Newsweek*, the Washington press corps, and major television networks during political campaigns. Tim wanted the job because of his love of culture and saw it as an opportunity to create a better understanding of the arts.

In his current position as media relations manager for the Indianapolis Symphony Orchestra, Tim handles media relations with the local, regional, national, and international press, along with telling the ISO story to the public. While the administrative side of the symphony operates like a typical corporation, the organization is quite innovative on its artistic and programming side. For example, the orchestra holds the Symphony Promenade, which is a spring festival of thematic classical music, and Symphony on the Prairie, where people relax on the ground with a picnic and enjoy the music. There is also the Yuletide Celebration. ISO was the first orchestra in North America to do a multidiscipline holiday show.

Tim handles the publicity for all of these events. He looks forward to coming to work each day because there are always new challenges in his job.

Performance Librarian—a Job with Music

While an administrative job supports the functioning of a symphony orchestra, the job of performance librarian involves working closely with the orchestra and the music. These librarians' comprehensive knowledge of music, combined with their library skills, helps them get music to the musicians. First, they obtain the music from the orchestra's library or buy or rent new music. Rented music must then be returned when the orchestra is no longer using it. Once the music is obtained, the performance librarian is responsible for getting the music ready for the orchestra by adding the bowings and all the different marks that are necessary. Often the librarian works with the conductor and soloists in the preparation of the music. The librarian must also attend all rehearsals and concerts at home and on tour to make sure that the music is handed out to each musician and then collected after each performance. This is definitely not a job with the regular hours of a music librarian in a library.

The number of jobs is obviously limited by the number of orchestras requiring this service. In smaller orchestras this job is handled part-time by one of the musicians. Most performance librarians are current or former musicians from the orchestra who have gained their library experience through courses.

Salaries. Pay for this position varies and depends greatly upon whether the librarian is also considered a member of the orchestra eligible for union benefits. Jobs with the major orchestras that perform year-round vary from $50,000 to $80,000 a year. Individuals with other orchestras that have a shorter performing season earn much less.

Performance Librarian for a Major Orchestra

Michael K. Runyon is the principal librarian for the Indianapolis Symphony Orchestra. He began playing the piano in first grade and later picked up the trumpet, French horn, and harmonica. During his high school years, Michael became interested in composition and began composing and arranging for the school swing choir and jazz band. He went on to study composition in college and says that most college programs allow the study of both classical composition—for symphonies, ballets, and operas— and commercial composition—for jingles, film scores, and television shows. He is equally versed in classical and commercial composition.

Throughout his college years, Michael worked as a copyist, arranger, and studio musician; he also played in bands, taught at universities, worked in art groups, and wrote grants. Michael holds bachelor's, master's, and a doctorate degrees in composition. Because of his musical background, he can customize parts for the orchestra and analyze scores for them. In recent years, Michael has taken time to perform solo harmonica with orchestras around the country.

Michael, with the help of one full-time and two part-time performance librarians, gets the parts ready for the individual symphony players. When the orchestra buys or rents music, it is never ready for the musicians' stands as it comes out of the package. Often the music has been written for more or fewer instruments than the Indianapolis Symphony has. Then decisions have to be made whether additional musicians will be brought in, whether some musicians will be allowed to go on holiday, or whether some musicians will be assigned extra parts. The principals of each section and the conductor mark the music to indicate changes so that everyone in each section will be reading the same music. Michael and the other performance librarians see that these changes are made for each musician.

As a performance librarian, Michael needs to be preparing music months in advance of its presentation as well as honing details for compositions soon to be performed. His duties also extend to working on cost analyses of proposed concerts and answering questions such as how many musicians will be needed and whether soloists will be required. Michael likes working with the production of a concert. He is able to handle the pressure of having the music be perfect for each musician when the conductor raises his baton. During symphony performances, Michael prefers to just sit out front and enjoy the music as a consumer rather than as a producer because he has done his part to make the music ready for the musicians.

Opera—Acting, Singing, and Music

Opera is a drama that brings music lovers beautiful music sung by sumptuous voices in elaborate settings. Because opera requires so many singers and musicians for a performance, it is very expensive to stage. The major problem of all opera companies is securing sufficient funds. In the United States, the most famous company is the Metropolitan Opera in New York City, which is also hoome to the New York City Opera. San Francisco, Boston, Chicago, Houston, Seattle, Los Angeles, Miami, and Washington, D.C., also have important opera companies. While many other cities have opera companies, they generally have short seasons and are likely to perform just a few operas a year.

Even though an opera audience only sees the performers, the orchestra, and the conductor, there is a large group of people behind the scenes who are needed to stage these complicated performances. Major opera companies have permanent organizations with general managers, music directors, stage directors, costume and set designers, administrative staff, technical staff (lighting electricians, sound engineers), production staff, props managers, construction crews, lighting crews, makeup artists, wardrobe handlers, stagehands, and ticket personnel. There is currently an all-time high demand for technical and production specialists. And there is always a need for outstanding fund-raisers and volunteers. In seeking a career as a behind-the-scenes professional, however, it is important to remember that many opera companies only have a small permanent administrative staff and few have year-round staffs.

Director of the San Francisco Opera Center

Outside of New York City, the opera company that gives the greatest number of performances is the San Francisco Opera. An important part of the success of the company lies in the San Francisco Opera Center. Its mandate is to train young emerging artists so they can make the transition from the university or conservatory level to professional roles and then can become either part of the San Francisco Opera or pursue other operatic options. As director of the opera center, Sheri Greenawald produces operas that allow these young artists to train by performing. For each opera, she has the responsibility of choosing a conductor, director, and set and costume designers as well as putting the singers in the right parts. Besides managing the training program, Sheri serves as an acting coach and director. In addition, she assists in raising funds to support the activities of the opera center.

Another Job Title. In her work at the San Francisco Opera, Sheri also serves as the artistic director of the Merola Opera Program. It is an eleven-week program designed to help launch the careers of gifted young talent, including singers, pianists, and stage directors from around the world. Entry into the program is highly competitive. The participants perform in two fully-staged operas and two semi-staged concerts. Sheri is in charge of every aspect of the performances, from selecting the operas to arranging for the teachers who guide the participants.

Career Path. Before coming to San Francisco, Sheri had a distinguished international operatic singing career as a soprano, singing an enormous range of roles. Not only has she sung featured roles with major opera companies, she has worked with most of opera's great conductors and directors. Her educational background includes being a graduate of the University of Northern Iowa and the Professional Studies Program at the Juilliard School of Music. In addition to her successful career as a singer, Sheri's resume includes this list of operatic positions:

- Visiting Artist, University of Charleston
- Artist in Residence, University of Northern Iowa
- Vocal Coach, Santa Fe Apprentice Program
- Program Director, Santa Fe Apprentice Program
- Master Classes Instructor, Opera Theatre of St. Louis
- Professor of Voice and Opera, Boston Conservatory

Because of her impressive credentials, the San Francisco Opera Company sought Sheri for the positions she now holds.

Career Advice. For positions like the ones Sheri now holds as head of two companies, you will need to have lived the life of a singer. Additional experience on the technical side is also helpful. Sheri points out that it is essential to immerse oneself in opera to find success in this field.

Fund-Raising—an Administrative Responsibility

Ticket sales cover less than half the operating costs for opera companies. Without an active fund-raising program, most companies would have to limit the number of operas presented as well as the education and outreach programs they offer. Because fund-raising is so important, the Development Department of the San Francisco

Opera company has nineteen employees. Under the director of development, the fund-raising program is split into these areas: annual giving, leadership giving, foundations and grants, corporate giving, and planned giving, or bequests. Together, these areas have the responsibility of raising $32 million every year.

Leadership (Major) Gifts Officer

Elizabeth Piper is a senior leadership gifts officer. Her job entails working with the large donors to make sure they have the best experience possible at the San Francisco Opera. This requires keeping a number of large donors happy by making sure that they are invited to the right events and honoring their various requests. In addition, her duties include prospecting and finding new donors and developing strategies on how to engage them with the opera. Fulfilling these responsibilities involves considerable phone and e-mail time as well as close collaboration with a committee of board members to work with the donors on their giving.

Career Path. Elizabeth always had a passion for opera and attended operas whenever she could, usually back in the standing-room section. She was a college graduate with experience in marketing, public relations, events management, and fund-raising when she heard about her present job from a friend of a friend who worked at the San Francisco Opera. Her path to a job in the arts came about through networking, a very effective way for music lovers to find appealing positions in the arts.

Career Advice. Elizabeth stresses the necessity for those seeking jobs in development to have a passion for the cause. Before taking a job with a nonprofit, she believes that it is a good idea to see what growth opportunities there are within the organization because the burnout rate for any fund-raising position is very high. If there are no opportunities available in development, Elizabeth advises getting started in a different area in the organization with the idea of moving over to development when the opportunity rises. Alternatively, you could find a fund-raising position with another cause and then move over to the arts.

The Publishing Side of Music

Adding to the diversity of jobs in the music world is the publishing side of music—including the publication of books and magazines on music, instruction books for different instruments, sheet music, and school textbooks. Music lovers who want to work in the book and magazine side of publishing can find a wide variety of jobs dealing with music because there are jobs for editors, writers, and marketing and sales people. Plus, there are magazines for almost every musical interest, so music lovers have the opportunity to spend their days working in some way with their favorite form of music, whether it is classical, country, opera, or heavy metal.

Publishing Sheet Music

Every piece of sheet music that musicians use has been published by a music publishing company. There are large publishing houses as well as small, independent music publishers. Many individuals start out with large companies and then leave these companies to start their own firms. Other publishing houses are launched by writers of hit tunes to sell their own music. No matter what their size, music publishing companies must select music that will sell. This is an important knack that determines how successful a company will be. One hit popular song can make a very large amount of money for a music publisher.

The same steps are followed in publishing sheet music regardless of a company's size. It begins with the evaluation of a music manuscript to determine the quality of the music and whether it is a fit for the publisher. If selected, a work is then engraved to prepare it for the printing process. It must then be copyrighted. The final step is the sales and marketing of the sheet music. To learn more about music publishing, contact:

Music Publishers' Association
243 Fifth Avenue, Suite 236
New York 10016
www.mpa.org

A Sheet Music Publisher

Scott Houston and his father found a unique marketing niche in the music publishing business. They became educational music publishers who sold band and choir arrangements for use in schools, instructional books for instruments, and manuscript paper. Their firm is small—just four employees. Scott has the responsibility of evaluating submissions from personal acquaintances and other people who know what type of music the company publishes. He contacts the writers of salable music and offers them standard royalty contracts. Next, the company obtains the copyright for the music. Then the music is sent out to a music engraving company, which prepares the piece for printing. Scott does the layout and the prepress production work, and the music is printed in-house. For sixteen weeks of the year, Scott and his father are on the road separately, going to conventions and visiting stores to let retailers know about their products.

Music Copyists—Preparing Sheet Music for Publication

Music copyists take each individual line of music from a full musical score and transfer that information onto a single part for individual musicians to perform. For example, a copyist goes through a complete score and writes out the entire part for the flute, making it much easier for the flutist to play the part. Traditionally, copying had been done with a special technical pen, with the same process followed for each musical instrument. Just as the computer has changed the way we work in other areas, it has revolutionized copying music. Copyists can now play on a keyboard directly into a computer. The information is then translated into printed notations. This is a very quick process, and, by using the computer, copyists can quickly send completed scores anywhere in the world to music publishers and other groups needing their work. Music copyists work for live performances, recording sessions, or music publishers. They either work independently or are associated with a copy house or music publisher.

Express Music Services

Lee Monroe is the owner of Express Music Services. He has been a full-time copyist for twenty-four years and was strictly a hand copyist for the first fifteen. His first experience with copying occurred when he did copy work for his composer roommate at Florida State University, where he was studying music. Then Lee moved to Orlando, Florida, to work as a professional trumpet player. He supplemented this income by working at Walt Disney World, where he really learned how to be a music copyist. Discovering that being a copyist paid far better than being a musician, he abandoned his musical performance career to become a full-time copyist.

With the introduction of computer music notation programs in the eighties, many musicians were reluctant to read off copy created on the computer because of the typeset look of the music fonts. Lee's company, as well as several others, created fonts from the hand-copy work of several professional music copyists, including his own. This, along with the improvement of music notation software, facilitated the transformation of the music copying industry to digital applications and allowed for direct interaction between MIDI music composition and music notation. Recognizing the possibilities for the future, Lee's company made the transformation practically overnight from hand copying to computer music notation in the midnineties; even though it would at times take considerable effort to learn how to create one measure of drum notation. Hand copyists had to have artistic ability; however, those using the computer need only to be comfortable with using a computer and be familiar with the music notation program.

Today, Lee's company has clients all over the world. He produces work primarily for recording sessions and not for mass production. With the advent of computerized copying, he has the ability to work up to the last minute while recording in London, Budapest, Los Angeles, or even Tokyo. He has a stable of independent music copyists and also works with other copy houses to print and deliver music parts to wherever his clients are recording.

Career Advice. You cannot expect to make a living as a copyist until you can produce practically flawless copy. To attain this level of skill, you should try to work with a top professional even if the pay is low or nonexistent. And whenever you have the opportunity, pick the brain of a good copyist in learning this skill. To find jobs, talk to every professional you can find. Try and learn which services are producing movies, traveling shows, recording sessions, and so on to find jobs.

Publishing School Music Textbooks

Schoolchildren do not just use textbooks for mathematics, history, and reading; they also use textbooks in their music classes. This is a specialized industry within music publishing because of the need to meet age-specific learning requirements. Because of the current cutback in music programs in schools, fewer music textbooks are now being purchased by school corporations, limiting the job opportunities in this area.

A Music Textbook Publisher

Larry Hillman was the executive editor for music at Silver Burdett and Ginn. In this position, he had the responsibility for both creating the company's music materials for kindergarten through eighth grade and for supervising a staff of fourteen editors—all of whom were musicians and former music teachers. As part of his job, Larry spoke with both teachers and students to determine what type of product each grade level needed. Dreaming up the product was the creative side of his job. The administrative side included supervising his department, making business projections, overseeing the budget, and directing sales and marketing efforts. An appealing aspect of this job for Larry was being in direct daily contact with music, since he supervised the recording of every song used in the series.

Career Path. In studying Larry's career path to his job as executive editor, music lovers can see other job opportunities they might like to explore. Larry's first job was as a music teacher. His qualifications for this job included playing the piano and organ since he was in second grade and holding both bachelor's and master's degrees in music. He also had a minor in business, which turned out to be very helpful in his career. After teaching music from kindergarten through junior college for ten years, Larry became a music consultant with Silver Burdett; this was both a sales and a service job. He presented the company's products to the teachers and then went back to help the teachers learn to use the materials after a school had purchased them. Larry was next promoted to product manager of music, essentially a marketing job. He had to come up with advertising campaigns and help oversee research and product development. Before becoming executive editor, Larry was a program editor who had supervising responsibilities and did direct editing of music materials.

The Recording Industry

The recording side of music represents a multibillion-dollar industry that produces all the CDs music lovers buy in order to listen to their beloved music. Today, there are more than two thousand companies producing and selling music, which adds up to a considerable number of jobs for music lovers. There are giant corporations that produce almost every type of music and have a large stable of artists. On the other hand, there are very small companies that may only produce one type of music or the music of a few artists.

The three leading cities for recording music are New York, Los Angeles, and Nashville, although companies are scattered throughout the United States. The largest companies have offices in several cities. Most no longer have recording studios, assigning this work to small studios close to the artists or their companies.

The making and selling of a recording is a complicated process. At the giant corporations, individuals work in a specific area such as promotion, marketing, sales, or publicity; at smaller companies, employees tend to have their hands in almost every aspect of producing and selling a recording. What follows is a description of the people who are involved in producing a recording and exactly what their roles are so that music lovers can see what jobs might appeal to them in the recording arena.

Artist and Repertoire Department (A&R)

A&R professionals work for record companies, for artists, or independently. They find talent as well as the music an artist or group will perform. The music may come from a staff writer, the artist or group, a new arrangement of an old favorite, or a demo sent to the company.

A&R works with the producer in planning all the details of the recording, from the number of musicians to choosing a recording studio. A&R is also in charge of the budget for a recording, which includes paying the bills and keeping financial records. In reality, A&R seems to be in on almost every decision about a recording. The department works with advertising, promotion, public relations, and marketing to determine the game plan for releasing a recording.

Art Department

The design of CD covers plays an important role in the selling of recordings. Designers, graphic artists, and photographers work on their creation. They may also design websites or contribute to the graphic look of advertising campaigns.

Promotion, Publicity, and Advertising

A well-integrated plan has to be developed to catch the eyes and ears of the prospective buyers of recordings. The greater the audience who reads, listens to, or hears about a new recording, the greater the chance it will be successful. This means getting radio stations to play the recording and talk show personalities and music critics to interview the artist or group, scheduling television appearances and press conferences, and buying advertisements in all the media. It may even include coming up with a gimmick such as a special T-shirt, pin, or hat.

Sales and Marketing

Marketing strategies have to be developed to get recordings into the hands of the consumer. This involves close work with promotion, publicity, and advertising as well as setting up displays in stores and visiting or calling stores, music directors at radio and television stations, and music columnists at newspapers and magazines. Music lovers desiring to work for large recording companies will find having a degree in some field of business or music helpful in securing a job. Working as an intern or in an entry-level position can give job seekers the experience most recording companies expect them to have. Jobs can be found through contacts in the field and ads in newspapers and trade papers such as *Billboard*, which is online at www.billboard.com.

Recording Studios and Recording Engineers

It has been said that there is a recording studio on almost every corner in Nashville. Recent advances in technology have made it possible for small studios to produce excellent sound recordings. Today, music is often recorded at certain studios because of the expertise of the recording engineers who work at, use, or own these studios. No matter how excellent an artist, band, or recording company, the success of a recording also depends on the end product the recording engineer creates.

Recording engineers operate the sophisticated equipment used to make recordings. Their job begins with setting up the equipment to produce the sound they want. During the actual recording session, they must push the right buttons and switches to get the desired sound. Finally, and this requires considerable skill, they must mix the many recorded tracks down to between two and five tracks. At times, a recording is made at several studios—even in different cities. For example, the rhythm track may be recorded in one studio and the vocals at another while the sound is mixed at yet another studio.

Some recording engineers hold bachelor's degrees in electrical engineering. Others may have completed courses at vocational technical schools, and some learn by serving as apprentices. There is a great deal of competition for positions as recording engineers. One of the best ways to secure a job is by serving as an intern. Although recording engineers may begin by earning no more than minimum wage, successful engineers working for name performers or groups can easily make $100,000 or more a year.

Aire Born

Mike Wilson and John Bolt are partners who own Aire Born, a recording studio located in the Midwest. They rent studio time plus their expertise as recording engineers. The two have created a successful business recording commercials, albums, and corporate materials. More than 50 percent of their work comes from servicing a small niche in the recording business—music publishers. These clients want recordings to demonstrate the sound of their sheet music to potential customers.

Mike and John traveled slightly different paths in becoming recording engineers, although both feel they gained their expertise through hands-on work experience. Mike obtained a degree in music business and went to a recording workshop during college. While in high school and later on, he played in a rock band that had its own eight-track recording studio, which gave him practical experience in sound recording.

John, on the other hand, went to a technical school as part of high school and took a course in sound engineering. After high school, he also attended a recording workshop. The workshop then offered him a job that gave John his work experience in the business. In his next job, he worked at a studio owned by a sacred-music writer and demonstrated his expertise by making recordings that earned three gold records in the religious market.

Mike and John met while working at different studios and quickly found that they shared similar values as well as the goal of owning a twenty-four-track recording studio. They decided to mortgage their homes and start Aire Born, which has proved to be a successful venture. Today, they have six other employees—two full-time engineers, a media editor, a studio manager, an office manager, and a bookkeeper.

The Bengemark for Music

Johann Sebastian Bach wrote music to order for patrons. In the same way, Doug Benge, owner of the Bengemark for Music, creates music for clients, usually advertisers and businesses seeking music for meetings and new product launches.

The first step involves talking to the client to find out what the music is to accomplish—the desired image or mood. Then Doug uses a computer program to compose a piece of music. The musical notation program transmits what he plays on a keyboard to notes he can see on the computer screen. Then without leaving his chair in front of the computer, Doug is able to assign his newly composed piece to different synthesizers using two software programs to create the music in a rough form. The client listens to the music, and any necessary changes are made before the final product is recorded. Composing has certainly changed since Bach's time.

Like Bach, this modern composer is a musician who shares a great love of music. Doug has an impressive academic background, with a bachelor's degree in philosophy and a master's in English. His music background includes playing in bands.

The Retail Side of Music

Music lovers are good customers of retail stores selling CDs, sheet music, and musical instruments and their accessories. These stores can also be pleasant places for them to work, with music frequently drifting through the air as they assist customers who share their interest in music, leading to many congenial conversations on different aspects of music.

Owners and managers of retail music and record stores must have a solid knowledge of music as well as of business. While a college education is not required, courses at this level can provide a good background in both music and business. Salespeople need to be knowledgeable about music and skilled in dealing with customers. If they work in a store selling instruments, it is a decided plus for them to be able to play one or more instruments.

Being a salesperson is a good way to enter the retail side of music. With experience, salespeople can advance to managerial positions or even to owning their own stores. Jobs at retail music stores are not limited to sales positions; many stores also offer repair services and lessons.

Musical Instrument Repairers

Music lovers are able to combine their love of music with a highly skilled craft in this very small profession. Almost all repairers have a strong musical background and an ability to play the instruments they repair so they can check their work. They also need to have a high level of skill and the ability to pay close attention to detail.

Repairers learn this trade through the few technical schools and colleges offering courses in instrument repair, through correspondence courses, and through jobs as assistants and apprentices. On the job, most repairers work alone in one of these four specialty areas: band instruments, pianos and organs, violins, and guitars. A few may work in more than one area. Repairers may work either full-time or part-time in their own businesses or for a retail or repair shop. Most repair work is done in shops, except for piano and organ repair.

Job Outlook and Salaries

The employment of musical instrument repairers is expected to increase more slowly than the average career. This is partly due to the cutback of school music programs due to budgetary concerns. Opportunities are best for those repairers who have received training from the few schools offering it. Earnings vary greatly depending on the expertise of the repairer. Median hourly earnings for all repairers are slightly more than $14.

For More Information

The National Association of Professional Band Instrument Repair Technicians (NAPBIRT) offers formal continuing education programs, technical clinics, a problem-solving service, annual conferences, technical clinics, self-evaluation programs, and industry evaluation. To learn more about this organization and a career in repairing band instruments, contact:

NAPBIRT
PO Box 51
2026 Eagle Road
Normal, IL 61761
www.napbirt.org

For information on piano tuning and repair work, contact:

Piano Technicians Guild
4444 Forest Avenue
Kansas City, KS 66106
www.ptg.org

Musical Instrument Makers

Some musical instrument makers have become famous for their skill in making the very finest musical instruments. Violinists are willing to pay thousands of dollars—in some cases millions—for violins made by Italian Renaissance violin maker Antonio Stradivari. As an instrument maker, you may make the entire instrument or work in collaboration with other craftspeople. You may specialize in the making of one instrument or in a range of instruments, usually from the same family, such as stringed, electronic, brass, woodwind, or percussion. Instrument makers may own their own shops or work in shops with other instrument makers. Some highly skilled instrument makers design instruments in consultation with musicians. Instrument makers often repair and restore musical instruments as well.

Instrument makers use skills that are also employed in cabinetmaking, metal pipe making, silversmithing, electrical wiring, and wood carving. They gain the needed skills through schooling and working with skilled instrument makers. On the personal side, they need to have good hand-eye coordination and hearing and an ear for musical pitch. It is also helpful if they can play the instrument they are making. This career requires patience and the ability to pay attention to the finest details. Plus, instrument makers should enjoy technical and engineering work.

Glamour Jobs in Music

You can combine your love of music with a glamorous career in the limelight or behind the scenes when you have a job in radio, television, and movies or working with rising stars and superstars. Perhaps you could be one of the many people in the background helping famous musicians like pop star Madonna or violinist Isaac Stern in their careers. On the other hand, you can grab part of the limelight for yourself with a job as a personality presenting music from country to classical on the radio, commenting on operas and symphonies to radio and television audiences, or even introducing music videos to MTV viewers.

Radio and Music

Wake up in the morning to the sound of music drifting from your clock radio. Hop in the car and drive with music easing the boredom. Jog along a path with music from the radio setting the rhythm of your stride. Wherever people go, their radios go with them, and, much of the time, the radios are tuned to music programs. Depending on the organization of a radio station, the individual selecting the music could be the program director, the music director, the on-air personality, or someone holding some combination of these titles. No particular educational requirements exist for these jobs; however, knowledge of music is definitely a prerequisite. Most people currently working at these positions began their careers in small radio stations working at any job they could find or through a college internship. The typical career ladder is from on-air personality position (also called disc jockey) to music director to program director and from small station to larger station at every job change.

Salaries. The pay for being an on-air personality in a major market can be quite good, according to those in the field; the average income for this position is currently $105,000 a year, with some earning much more. It all depends on the ranking of the jockey's particular station and each specific market (how many listeners a program has). In the top three markets—New York, Chicago, and Los Angeles—the top three or four morning personalities easily make more than a million dollars. Other major-market disc jockeys, depending on their time slot, make in the range of $30,000 to $60,000 a year. Pay is even good in smaller markets, ranging from $25,000 to $40,000 a year.

Unfortunately, there is now a trend for large station conglomerates to run "jockless" stations—music preprogrammed and run by computer with only a single person providing station-imaging announcements. These automated stations are only moderately successful in the marketplace, but they don't have to pay salaries.

Morning Personality

Scott Fischer was the morning personality of WENS in Indianapolis, working the 6 A.M. to 10 A.M. shift. During the ten years he was at WENS, it was an all-music station. Sometimes Scott cannot believe that he was paid to have such fun in the morning.

Music has always played an important role in this music lover's life. As a child, Scott collected and listened to records, besides playing the mellophone and French horn. It seemed natural for him to select a career that combined music with his other love—radio. In college, Scott majored in theater and communications, a useful background for individuals seeking employment in radio. However, Scott really got his first exposure to the radio business in college by working at the campus radio station and a local radio station on weekends and during the summer.

After graduation, Scott spent several months scouring the smaller radio markets for a job as a disc jockey, sending his resume and demo tape to stations. While most on-air personalities begin their careers at small-market stations working for salaries close to minimum wage, Scott secured a job in a medium-market station in Des Moines. From Des Moines, he went to Denver to work as on-air personality and music director for more money and in a better time slot—a typical career move for on-air personalities. After Denver, Scott worked in major-market radio stations in Chicago and Atlanta before securing his job in Indianapolis.

Like all successful on-air personalities, Scott has a warm and friendly voice which he can adapt to dozens of different situations—from over-the-edge excitement to overly mellow and everything in between. He left the radio show to pursue his promo voice-over career. Although he misses being on the air, he is delighted to be the promo voice of so many news, sports, and weather programs and special events.

On-Air Personality and Music Director

J. D. Cannon of WFMS in Indianapolis, a country radio station, was given the Large Market Personality of the Year award in 1998 and again in 2004 by the Country Music Association. His expertise as an on-air personality was further recognized by his induction into the Country Music DJ Hall of Fame in 2002. J.D. prepared for his career as an on-air personality by attending a vocational-technical school and studying broadcasting for a year. Part of the curriculum at the school was technical training, and part was announcing. J.D. learned about his first job from another student at the school who told him about an ad for an afternoon news anchor at a Madison, Wisconsin, radio station. From this job, J.D. went on to become an on-air personality at the station.

In his current job, J.D. is also the music director, a position that requires the ability to judge and predict which new songs will become popular with listeners. Each week, J.D. sifts through approximately fifty new songs to select the four or five that will be added to the rotation at his station. This is a time-consuming job that begins on Monday, when he spends two or three hours on the phone talking to promoters. On Tuesday, he enters all the music into the computer to create the computer-generated play list for the week. J.D. categorizes the songs according to current popularity so the computer program can generate the printed list that details when and how often songs will be played. J.D. uses information from research companies, music charts, and publications such as *Radio & Records*, *Billboard*, and the *Gavin Report* to determine which songs are hot locally and which songs are starting to lose popular appeal. On Wednesday, he listens to all of the new products and decides which ones to insert in his previously adjusted computer list.

Because J.D. is an on-air personality, he must also spend time each day preparing for his daily program, which includes chitchat about music and information on artists and concerts between segments of nonstop music. In addition, he spends time making commercials for the program. Away from the radio station, J.D., like other on-air personalities, spends considerable time making personal appearances at parades and shopping malls.

Program Director

Ed Lennon held a wide variety of jobs—from selling cars to owning a fire alarm company—before he began working in radio part-time selling ads. Quickly, the radio bug bit, and Ed found he was spending more time at the station fooling with the equipment and writing and producing commercials than selling ads. His next job was as a part-time producer of a radio show at another station. He proved himself by working forty- and fifty-hour weeks at his part-time job. Soon he was pushing the buttons and cuing up the records for Dick Clark's syndicated show.

At every opportunity, Ed always volunteered and took on more responsibility, which led to a temporary full-time position producing commercials and then to the job of production director responsible for the production of all commercials and promotions at the station. Being willing to work hard throughout his entire career helped Ed obtain a job as program manager for WIBC—a large station in a major market area where he supervised the on-air staff and directed the on-air sound, which included choosing the right music for WIBC's audiences.

A Music Critic

Imagine the satisfaction for a music lover of being involved vicariously with music through writing about concerts, reviewing records and CDs, and interviewing music presenters and musicians. This is the job that Jay Harvey enjoyed as a classical and jazz music critic for the *Indianapolis Star*. With a background of trombone playing, a bachelor's degree in English, and a master's in teaching, Jay entered the teaching profession. After a few years, he decided on a different career path and went into newspaper work. For fifteen years, he reviewed classical music, visual arts programs, and some theater productions for the *Flint Journal* in Michigan.

He also wrote book reviews and general features for the paper. Wishing to concentrate on music, Jay moved to his current newspaper as a music critic.

A typical workday, which began at 2 P.M., might involve writing a review of *Porgy and Bess*, which he saw the previous evening; completing a piece on the labor and management problems of the local symphony orchestra; listening to recordings sent to him to review; and writing short announcements about music activities throughout the state. During a usual work week, Jay would attend three or four musical performances, illustrating the varying days and hours that music critics work.

With staff changes at the paper, Jay's work as a music critic became the niche beat of jazz. He also is working on the copy desk and doing arts and entertainment reporting.

Job Qualifications and Outlook. Job requirements for the position of music critic on a newspaper include having a good ear and an excellent knowledge of music and the contemporary music scene, as well as strong writing skills. Besides finding jobs at newspapers, music critics also work for music-industry magazines. At the present time, career opportunities for newspaper music critics are limited. Huge cuts are being made in the staffs at newspapers, and most have turned to freelancers to reduce expenses.

Managing Musical Stars and Groups

A personal manager is a deal maker who oversees all aspects of an individual's or a group's musical career. This involves dealing with record companies, music publishers, booking agents, and merchandisers. It also means handling the promotion, publicity, touring, and concert logistics for the artist or group. Then there is the all-important job of managing the money. Finally, the personal manager must work constantly to develop the group's career and an audience for the group's music. For handling this wide variety of jobs, a manager makes from 10 to 50 percent of gross income; the typical manager takes from 15 to 20 percent. Working with a top artist or group can mean an income of more than $500,000 a year. Most personal managers usually handle one artist or group. The trend today, however, is toward companies that handle several artists or groups and divide the responsibilities among a staff of professionals. There are not a lot of one-on-one relationships. The best way to find a job with one of these companies is by working as an intern.

The one qualification successful personal managers have in common is an excellent knowledge of how the music industry works. Contacts within the industry are also extremely important in launching and maintaining an act's career. Furthermore, personal managers must have a very good personal relationship with the individual artist or with the members of the group. At one time almost all personal managers were located in New York, Los Angeles, or Nashville. While this is where most managers still are, many personal managers now live in the same area as their artists or groups.

A Star Manager

If you are familiar with the rock hit, "Hey Baby," then you know that Henry Lee Summer is the artist responsible for this song. The personal manager who helped Henry Lee Summer go all the way to the top is James Bogard, who brought his considerable knowledge of the music industry to this task.

During high school, James had his first introduction to the industry when he played in a professional band. After graduation from the Berklee College of Music in Boston, he learned even more about the music world as a performer with a soul group that crisscrossed the country for more than five years. During this time, he acted as the eleven-member group's liaison with their manager, who taught him what was involved in being a manager through almost daily phone calls. James also had the opportunity to learn how to deal with nightclub owners, public relations people, and booking agents. After the group broke up, James became the manager of the band's rhythm section and got a new band up and working, to the point of being offered a recording contract, but he could not keep the group together.

James then worked at a recording studio where he met artists who wanted to make their own records, including Henry Lee Summer. Henry Lee impressed James because he had talent, drive, and determination to go to the top. James left the studio and concentrated on Henry Lee—helping him with his records, booking his nightclub act, and working on recording projects. Then he became Henry Lee's personal manager, handling all aspects of this rising artist's career, including arranging for his client to be interviewed on popular television shows by personalities such as David Letterman and overseeing the companies Henry Lee owned. Top artists like Henry Lee usually have their own publishing, touring, and production companies and may have record and even movie companies. Daily, James dealt with all the people who wanted to work with Henry Lee. He had an assistant who handled Henry Lee's personal financial planning and investments. When Henry Lee changed his career direction and no longer performed, James's own career took another direction into computers.

Booking Entertainers for Special Events

Joe Deal is owner of Joe Deal Events, a company that does special event planning. His company handles every aspect of an event and can even come up with the theme or promotional idea for the function. Joe has a roster of talent that includes bands, musicians, and entertainers of all types. He matches what his clients are looking for with the talents from the roster.

Joe obtained a bachelor of science degree in a music business program. This is a relatively new degree program, which Joe liked because he could combine his love of music with business courses. To get this degree he needed not only four years of study in college, but he also had to complete two internships. He did one at a booking agency and the other at a music store.

Music Careers in Places of Worship

In churches and temples, music is an important part of religious worship, from the rhythm of African drums to the melodic voices of the Mormon Tabernacle Choir. For music lovers who have a knowledge of church music and a desire to work in a religious setting, there are jobs for music directors and choir directors. Qualifications for these jobs usually include a bachelor's or master's degree in music plus an ability to direct music performers. Full-time jobs in these positions are often limited to churches and temples having large congregations. About the only other jobs in this area are as assistants to music and choir directors.

A Director of Music

Robert M. McBain served for many years as director of music at Carmel Methodist Church. He has bachelor's and master's degrees in music as well as a doctoral degree in musical arts (D.M.A.). In addition, he has an instrumental conducting degree from the Mozarteum in Salzburg, Austria, and has done postdoctoral study with Donald Neuen at the Eastman School of Music in Rochester, New York.

As the son of a Baptist minister and an accomplished vocalist, Robert's first association with music was closely linked to his involvement in church music programs. Today, he has strong personal feelings about sharing his musical talent with his church. Throughout his years of study, Robert stayed involved with church music and also worked in the school system teaching choral music in secondary schools. Even though he was director of music, supervising all the music programs in a large church, he was also a general vocal music teacher in the public schools. Robert wants music lovers who are thinking of becoming church music directors to realize that it may be necessary to supplement their incomes, as he has done through the years with his teaching.

As director of music at a church with twenty-six hundred members, Robert managed a staff that included a part-time children's choir director, a full-time organist, and a music associate. Besides the paid staff members, there were also a number of volunteers. Robert has been the music director of several other churches and has had staffs of fifty people reporting to him as well as being the only musician on staff. In many churches, the music director is also the choir director and organist.

In addition to his responsibilities as church music director and teacher, Robert was also director and conductor of the 150-member Carmel Symphonic Chorale and executive director of Music at Carmel, Inc., which puts on monthly concerts for the community. In the past, this versatile musician has been guest conductor at symphony orchestras in Oklahoma, Phoenix, Atlanta, and Indianapolis. He has also been the bass soloist for Robert Schuller's "Hour of Power," sung with the Robert Shaw Choral, and recorded several albums.

Salaries. The salary for directors of music varies greatly depending on the organization. For example, in some large churches in major cities music directors can earn as much as $100,000 annually. At the same time, the average salary for music directors in church settings is slightly less than $20,000 a year. And many directors have part-time jobs with salaries starting as low as $4,000 a year.

Choir Directors

Choir directors have the responsibility of directing the choir for church services. Directors also hold auditions for positions in the choir and work with section leaders, assistant conductors, and soloists. They must select music, direct weekly rehearsals, plan special programs, and work closely with the other members of the music staff of the church.

According to the National Association for Music Education, choir directors must have an ability to work with people, a commitment to religion and religious music, musical talent, and organizational skills. While a degree in sacred music is not required, equivalent training and professional certification is necessary. Salaries range from $5,200 to $70,000 a year.

A Cantor

A cantor is a unique combination of minister, music director, teacher, and chief soloist in a synagogue. Janice Roger became a cantor because of her desire to express her love of Judaism through music. As a cantor, she is involved with music at all liturgical services for the public and in all areas of the life cycle—birth, marriage, and death.

Janice's background includes a bachelor's degree in music and a bachelor's degree in sacred music from a seminary, where she studied music for the synagogue as well as philosophy and religion. Immediately upon graduation from the seminary, Janice became a cantor for a large congregation. Her career satisfaction comes from watching young people grow and develop Jewish identities. She believes a cantor most visibly helps members of congregations by elevating their spiritual lives through music.

The requirements for becoming a cantor are not consistent. It may or may not be necessary to have attended a seminary. The employment outlook for cantors is good because there are many more positions than there are people to fill them. According to the National Association for Music Education, cantors earn an annual salary between $75,000 and $150,000.

More Job Information for Music Lovers

The possibilities for finding a job associated with music are much greater than most people imagine. For example, whenever music lovers hear music, they should ask themselves where the music came from and who wrote, sold, marketed, or packaged the music. They also should investigate possible jobs in such areas as background music, telephone music, the military, and music technology.

Music lovers can also learn more about job opportunities by visiting the websites of organizations associated with music, from recording companies to symphonies to operas. Here are some organizations that you may wish to contact:

American String Teachers Association
National School Orchestra Association
4153 Chain Bridge Road
Fairfax, VA 22030
www.astaweb.com

Association of Performing Arts Presenters
1112 Sixteenth Street NW, Suite 400
Washington, DC 20036
www.artspresenters.org

Music Critics Association of North America
722 Dulaney Valley Road, #259
Baltimore, MD 21204
www.mcana.org

Music Teachers National Association
441 Vine Street, Suite 505
Cincinnati, OH 45202
www.mtna.org

National Music Publishers Association
101 Constitution Avenue NW, Suite 705 East
Washington, DC 20001
www.nmpa.org

Opera America
330 Seventh Avenue, Sixteenth Floor
New York, NY 10001
www.operaamerica.org

Recording Industry Association of America
1330 Connecticut Avenue NW, Suite 300
Washington, DC 20036
www.riaa.com

CHAPTER FOUR

Career Opportunities for Dance Lovers

Working with Ballet, Ballroom, Theater, and Other Forms of Dance

Will you, won't you, will you, won't you, will you join the dance?
—Lewis Carroll, *Alice's Adventure in Wonderland*

O f all the art forms, dance is the oldest. Primitive people drew pictures on cave walls in Spain depicting people dancing more than fifty thousand years ago. Many cultures have folk dances that have been passed down from generation to generation and are still being performed, like the Highland fling of Scotland, the German polka, and American folk dances. Dance is considered the mother of other arts. The first music was created as a rhythm for early dances. Artists and sculptors through the ages have been inspired to create masterpieces showing the grace of dancers. And it is believed that the drama traditions of most countries originated in their dances.

Dancing is fun for children and adults. It is the language of the body that lets us show our feelings and thoughts through movement. Children can't stay still when they hear the beat of music, nor can many adults who dance for the pure joy of moving their bodies to music. Today, more than ever before, people are viewing professional performances of dance and participating in dance activities, from lessons to social dancing to dance exercise classes. Dance continues to play a major role in our culture.

Because dance is currently so popular, there are good opportunities for careers associated with dancing. Dance lovers do not need to be performers to find careers involved with dancing. Teachers are needed at all levels, from preschool dance classes to classes for professional dancers. Choreographers are needed to design the movements that go with the music in different dances. Dance performances are enhanced by the individuals who create the costumes, scenery, and lighting. Dance therapists work in hospitals, clinics, and other rehabilitation centers to help injured dancers and athletes regain movement. Movement analysts help people eliminate poor movement habits and get rid of muscle tension by teaching them neuromuscular reeducation techniques. Dance historians, critics, and writers are needed at libraries, dance companies, and newspapers and magazines to communicate their knowledge of dance to the public. There are even dance medicine assistants—trainers, nurses, and doctors who use their knowledge of anatomy and understanding of body movements as they relate to dance to help restore people to improved health. Without question, there are countless jobs for dance lovers. At the same time, you must realize that few of them are nine-to-five jobs, since so many are associated with performances.

Choreographers

Choreographers create new dances and dance productions, modify or adapt existing dances, and integrate dance sections into shows. They are to dance what composers are to music. The choreographer is the key person in a dance company. It is the choreographer's job to know what the human body can do and to use that knowledge to teach the dancers how to move their bodies in the performance of a dance. The choreographer also works with the dance company's costume designer and lighting director to produce an integrated performance.

Most choreographers are self-taught. They learn to choreograph from their own personal dance experiences or by watching other choreographers work. Choreographers draw upon their own experiences to come up with ideas for dances. At times, the music provides the idea; at other times, the movement comes first and the music is added later. Choreographers must possess more than a knowledge of dance and music. They need to understand lighting, stage dimensions, and cameras. Their jobs vary from company to company. However, choreographers are usually expected to teach the company dance class, choreograph pieces for the company, rehearse the dancers, choose the dance repertoire, and select guest choreographers to work with the company.

Job Opportunities

Choreographers face intense competition for jobs. The number of applicants far exceeds the number of job openings. There are opportunities with large dance companies, but many small and midsize organizations present fewer opportunities because of reduced funding. Choreographers can also find work with opera companies; movie, television, and video productions; theaters; and nightclub shows.

New avenues are opening up for choreographers. For example, in the area of ice dancing, choreographers help skaters perform more exquisite patterns on the ice and in the air. Roller skating is another area in which choreographers are able to help coordinate movements to the music. With innovations such as electronic sounds and music videos, choreography is becoming an even more challenging career for talented and creative individuals.

Salaries

Earnings of choreographers with musical theater companies are specified by the Society of Stage Directors and Choreographers.

Choreographers of Broadway shows receive a weekly fee, an advance, and a minimum royalty. Fees for off-Broadway productions, nonprofit productions, and stock productions vary depending upon such things as the size of the theater and the length of the engagement. Earnings from fees and performance royalties range from about $1,000 a week in small professional theaters to more than $30,000 for an eight- to ten-week rehearsal period for a Broadway production. In high budget films, choreographers make $3,000 for a five-day week; in television, $7,500 to $10,000 for up to fourteen workdays.

Salaried choreographers have average annual earnings of close to $30,000. However, the lowest 10 percent earn less than $14,000 while the highest 10 percent earn more than $58,000 a year. Choreographers covered by union contracts are entitled to some paid sick leave, paid vacations, and various health and pension benefits.

Notators and Reconstructors

Ballet companies throughout the world often want to reproduce the work of a great choreographer even though the choreographer may be either deceased or simply unable to come and train their dancers. Since the 1920s, it has been possible to record every movement of a ballet because a system of dance notation was developed. This system, known as labanotation, uses special symbols to record every movement of a ballet. Special training is necessary to learn this symbol system. Many universities offer training in labanotation. For an opportunity to actually read a dance, visit the website of the Dance Notation Bureau, where you can learn more about how labanotation is actually done.

Notators used to produce the score of a dance with pencil and a ruler. Then an autographer would hand copy the score in ink or with a typewriter. With the advent of the computer, notators are now able to use a program to record each step, and the need for autographers is rapidly disappearing.

Individuals who can read a completed score and teach it to dancers are called reconstructors. Most reconstructors are college professors who do the work of restaging dances as freelancers. There is a very limited demand for the specialized skills of notators and reconstructors. For more information, contact:

Dance Notation Bureau
151 West Thirtieth Street, Suite 202
New York, NY 10001
http://dancenotation.org

Dance Companies

When dance lovers think of working for a dance company, they may immediately think of well-known companies such as New York City Ballet, American Ballet Theater, the Joffrey Ballet, San Francisco Ballet, or Alvin Ailey American Dance Theater. While these organizations have many jobs for dance lovers, a great number can also be found with smaller companies located in almost every region of the United States. To find where some of these dance companies are located, job seekers should consult *Stern's Performing Arts Directory* at a public library.

Dance Kaleidoscope

Dance lovers in Indiana have found satisfying jobs with Dance Kaleidoscope, a contemporary dance company started in 1972. The eleven-member company presents four subscription series a year. When members are not on stage, they perform for schoolchildren. The company also performs nationwide on tour. During the summer, Dance Kaleidoscope is in residence at the Oregon Shakespeare Festival, where they perform before productions and give contemporary views of various works of Shakespeare.

Because this company is small, staff members may do several jobs that would be handled by different individuals at a larger company. Full-time staff on the administrative side includes an executive director, director of marketing, a director of education and ticket coordinator, and a director of development. On the artistic side, there is an artistic director and a lighting designer. Other employees include a full-time costume mistress and a part-time costume designer who works as needed.

Artistic Director

David Hochoy is the artistic director of Dance Kaleidoscope and is therefore responsible for the way the company looks during a performance. He has to make sure that everything happens as scheduled and that all the elements run together smoothly to make the correct technical and artistic presentation. David also teaches the company's daily dance class, choreographs dances for the company, rehearses the dancers, chooses the company's repertoire, selects guest choreographers, and works with the lighting designer, production manager, technical director, and costume designer.

Because the company is small, David must do many other jobs. One of the most important is going out into the community to tell people about Dance Kaleidoscope. David envisioned what this company would be like and what it was going to become. He publicizes this vision with every form of media available so that the vision will become a reality. David also serves as a figurehead for the company for fund-raising activities.

Career Path. During his high school years, David became deeply involved with the arts as he studied piano, participated in the school choir, drew and painted, was a member of theater groups, participated in some theatrical productions, and entered public speaking contests. In college, he obtained a master's degree in theater but then decided against getting a doctorate because he preferred being a performer to being a member of the academic community. Knowing that he wanted to be a dancer, David went to New York City—dance center of the United States with the greatest number of dance companies. For several years, his life was a combination of working as a waiter at night and taking dance classes during the day. Then he took different jobs with small dance companies in New York and worked in Toronto for a year before joining the Martha Graham Dance Theater, where he stayed for ten years. He began with the company as an ordinary dancer, became a soloist, and then worked as a rehearsal director. In this position, David was no longer dancing; instead, he was directing the other dancers through their rehearsals. At the same time, he was also doing his own choreography and making his own dances. He became more interested in choreography and decided to leave the company to go to Texas Christian University in Fort Worth, Texas, the first university in the country to have a department for ballet and modern dance. Before this department was created, dancers had to study in a conservatory rather than on a university campus. For two years, as an assistant professor, David taught modern dance techniques, composition, and dance repertoire while choreographing and supervising student productions and counseling students.

A Challenging Job. Today, David finds his job at Dance Kaleidoscope to be challenging. He compares it to overcoming the obstacles in climbing Mt. Everest and finds it just as rewarding. This is the only job that David is interested in doing, even if he is on call twenty-four hours a day. He usually works an eight- to twelve-hour day; however, the closer it gets to a performance, the hours increase, and it is not uncommon for him to put in sixteen-hour days. In his free time, David loves to watch other dance companies. He listens to music all the time because he is always trying to find new music to use in choreographing a new number for the dance company.

From Director of Operations to Executive Director

Today, Jan Virgin is the executive director of Dance Kaleidoscope. Previously her job title had been director of operations. Most of the responsibilities that were hers as operations director are still hers. Whether Jan can hire additional staff affects the number of hats that she must wear. She hires staff when necessary, fires or lays off if needed, assesses staff work, and conducts yearly evaluations.

As executive director, she oversees the administrative aspects of the company—development, marketing, education, and touring. When any one of these areas lacks personnel or has problems, Jan steps in and takes control or leads with a heavier hand. She does not micromanage. Being involved in the financial aspects of Dance Kaleidoscope, however, is Jan's main concern. She works not only toward yearly financial stability but also toward growth through support and eventually having an endowment. She is also directly involved in all areas of developed income, whether it is preparing an original request for funding or demonstrating the company's appreciation of gifts. Getting more income for the dance company involves grant writing and reporting and donor campaigns that include individual and corporate events. Jan also watches her company's expenses, which includes budgeting (creating and working within the budget), paying the bills, and working closely with an accountant.

Director of Operations. A look at the responsibilities that Jan had as director of operations will give you a better idea of many of the tasks that she is still doing today. In her former job, she was expected to oversee all aspects of the day-to-day management of the administrative office, including budget, communication between board and staff, meetings pertaining to office operations, systems maintenance, and correspondence and reports as needed. Additionally, this position required her to coordinate staff and volunteer support for the lobby and the Dance Kaleidoscope boutique at concerts.

With such a broad job description, Jan found herself doing a variety of tasks each day and still does. Because she typically arrived first each morning, her day began as she turned on the equipment to get the office ready. During the course of the day, she might handle such tasks as proofing programs, making badges, hiring new employees, acting as the secretary at board meetings, monitoring supplies, handling complimentary ticket requests, making deposits, soliciting advertising for the season program, maintaining records regarding subscriptions and single-ticket sales, getting mailings out, and generally seeing that the Dance Kaleidoscope office was running smoothly. On performance days, her job extended to supervising the ushers and the operation of the boutique booth in the lobby.

Career Path. Throughout her life, Jan has been an avid culture lover. She learned to appreciate classical music from her father, a concert pianist who filled their home with music. And she was only five when her love of dance emerged and she began to take ballet lessons, which she continued for thirteen years. In college, Jan concentrated on training in medicine because her family wished her to have a more solid career than they believed she could have in the arts.

For a number of years after college, she worked in medicine and then as a special education and reading teacher. When one of her children, a talented dancer, began to tour with a dance company, Jan returned to the arts. Not only did she act as a chaperone for her daughter, she also danced professionally with the company in bit parts. Then she became a full-time administrative assistant for the ballet company and was the assistant marketing, development, and box office manager before leaving to become director of operations and then executive director of Dance Kaleidoscope.

Jan's job requires her to work closely with the artistic director, David Hochoy, and the dancers, which she appreciates as a true dance lover. At Dance Kaleidoscope she feels that she is part of a team in which each member—whether on the artistic or business side—appreciates everyone's contribution to the success of the company.

Director of Education and Ticket Coordinator

In her job with Dance Kaleidoscope, Lynn Webster wears two hats, as is typical in smaller dance companies. Lynn is both the director of education and the ticket coordinator. Eighty percent of her time is spent working as the education director, which she truly enjoys as the company is so focused on making children aware of the arts.

Dance Kaleidoscope evolved from the Young Audiences of Indiana program, which links the arts to schoolchildren, and still has a partnership with this organization. During the year, the company presents many in-school programs to acquaint children with dance. Also, the company is active in bringing students to shows and giving them an in-depth look at the performers. As director of education, Lynn is in charge of getting schools involved in the arts through the dance company's activities. Part of her job lies in finding sponsorships so more programs can be offered. Lynn is also actively involved in helping adults learn more about dance through community outreach and adult programs. The arts have always played a role in Lynn's life. Her mother was a dancer and her father was a musician.

Before becoming ticket coordinator, Lynn was Dance Kaleidoscope's first ticket manager. Then she was actively involved in the printing and mailing of tickets. Today, as ticket coordinator, she coordinates all the ticketing between Dance Kaleidoscope and the company that handles the actual printing and mailing.

Costume Designer

Barry Doss was a resident freelance costume designer for Dance Kaleidoscope for several years until he left for New York City to work on Broadway musicals and for costuming firms. In the dance company, he worked with David Hochoy, the artistic director of Dance Kaleidoscope, to create the appropriate costume designs for each performance. Because he worked with dancers, Barry had to make sure that the costumes would not only have artistic value but first and foremost be functional for freedom of movement. Costumes are different for different types of dancing, and the designer must know exactly what is needed. For example, because in ballet there is only limited movement of the upper torso, many costumes designed for the ballerina even have metal stays, while costumes for modern dance need to be designed so that the torso is free to move.

The Steps in Designing Costumes. As a costume designer, Barry watches the choreographer work with the dancers to get a design concept. The first step is to draw sketches to turn what the director wants into two-dimensional images that will give Barry a reference point from which he can work. The reference point shows lines and colors and actual shapes. In the artistic world, such a drawing is called a rendering.

After the costume designer and the choreographer come to an agreement on a rendering, the fabric needs to be selected. Samples are gathered and brought back to the director for approval. Once the fabric selection has been made, a pattern must be cut or draped. Muslin is used to drape and cut the pattern out directly on the form. Once the pattern is cut, it is used to cut out the material. At Dance Kaleidoscope, Barry did all of this himself. In a larger company, he would have assistants.

After the garment has been constructed, it is then fitted on the dancer so that the costume designer can check that it allows freedom of movement. Alterations can be made easily at this point. Then the costume is ready for the final sewing, followed by the finishing work. Finishing work means adding all the trim, glitter, rhinestones, buttons, snaps, and hooks and eyes that are needed for the costume. With the finishing work complete, the costume is ready for the dancer to come in for a final fitting.

On performance night at Dance Kaleidoscope, Barry could be found backstage if he was needed. However, he preferred to sit out front enjoying the show and seeing how all the hours of hard work had paid off. Costumes look different in the costume studio than when they are on the dancers under the stage lights, so Barry has to make sure that when the curtain goes up on a performance, everything is just as he and the director planned it.

Career Path. Barry holds a bachelor of arts in theater, with a double emphasis in acting performance and costume design and a minor in interior and fashion design. He attended college on an acting scholarship in theater at Texas Christian University. In college, Barry became actively involved in ballet and costuming when he worked on the ballet *Scheherazade*. He was the assistant designer for the production, which in this case meant doing most of the accessory work, such as headpieces.

At the university, he met David Hochoy and was so impressed with his choreography in *Starry Night*, a production based on the van Gogh painting with Philip Glass music, that he offered to work for David anytime he needed a costume designer. Barry got the chance to work with him at the school on *Young Apollo*, a production set to Nat King Cole's music. Barry had to design four costumes for the production—costumes for a young man and three muses. Since *Young Apollo* is a mythical piece with a modern twist, the muses had to look like goddesses—but not in the traditional sense. To achieve this difficult assignment, Barry used a lot of color.

In his free time, this culture lover enjoys going to the theater, history and art museums, and large spectacular musical shows such as *Les Misérables*. He also enjoys shopping for antiques, going to arts and crafts shows, and attending dance performances. From all of these visual experiences, he is able to gather ideas and inspirations for his own work. Barry feels that being a costume designer requires versatility. During your schooling, he suggests you study costume designing for dance, theater, films, television, and commercials before choosing an area in which to specialize.

More Jobs with Dance Companies

At one time, dance lovers would have had trouble finding jobs with dance companies outside of New York and other major cities such as Chicago and San Francisco. Now there are hundreds of small companies. Unfortunately, these companies do not have large staffs of administrators. When they first start, many just have a director, but as they win acclaim they add general managers; marketing, development, and operations staff; accountants; and other administrative support. Some companies don't hire their own staffs but obtain the management help they need from a company that offers support services to several dance or other performing arts companies. Dance lovers should also consider jobs with these firms.

Teaching Dance—Training Dance Lovers

Children just naturally dance; they can hardly keep their bodies still. Throughout their lives, most people continue loving to dance. Millions of dollars are spent every year for dance lessons for preschoolers learning to tap and do ballet, for high school students learning social dancing, and for adults brushing up on their ballroom dance steps or simply exercising through dance. Professional ballet dancers even take lessons or daily practice classes to stay in top physical condition. Teachers are needed to train all of these eager dancers in a variety of settings, such as day care centers, nursing homes, state hospitals, public schools, dance schools, colleges, studios, conservatories, and special education programs. Your dream of teaching dance can even extend to owning your own dance studio. Job opportunities appear to be best for dance lovers seeking employment as dance teachers in private studios and schools.

Teaching dance gives dance lovers an opportunity not only to be closely involved with dance but to actually dance on the job. Do you think that you possess the necessary special skills and knowledge to be a dance teacher? Ask yourself the following questions:

1. Do you have an anatomical understanding of how the body works?
2. Do you have the ability to relate to people of different ages?
3. Do you enjoy music?
4. Do you have the ability to choreograph dances for other people?
5. Do you have the patience to teach the same step over and over?
6. Do you have the organizational skills needed to break a dance down into parts and then reteach each part until the whole dance has been mastered?
7. Do you have the skills necessary to keep discipline in a class?
8. Do you possess a sense of rhythm?
9. Are you able to express ideas, moods, and emotions through dance movements?
10. Are you self-confident?
11. Are you creative?
12. Are you able to work under pressure at times?
13. Do you have ambition?
14. Do you have talent?
15. Are you willing to spend long hours in training and practice?
16. Do you have good physical endurance?
17. Do you have leadership ability?
18. Do you have a sincere interest in and love of dancing?

Dance lovers truly qualified to become dance teachers typically answer yes to nearly every one of the above questions. To actually teach dance, the training and educational background needed depend on the type of dance you wish to teach and where you want to teach. Many private dance teachers have trained since early childhood, and their own personal background acts as the foundation of their teaching. Most of these dancers continue their own lessons and practice sessions even after they have started to teach dance. Dance lovers who want to teach in a public school, however, need to have bachelor's degrees and credentials just like other teachers in the educational system. Having experience as a performer is often a requirement for dance teachers.

Earnings

The average salaries of teachers in private practice vary widely, depending on the number of hours they work and the places of employment. Salaries range between $10,000 and more than $30,000 a year. Dance teachers in public schools and colleges earn the same salaries as other teachers.

A Dance Teacher with His Own Studio

The Arthur Murray International Dance Organization has a network of more than two hundred franchised dance studios in the United States. Russell Clark is the organization's master franchisee of Puget Sound. He owns one studio and is affiliated with others. Previously, he owned a studio in Indianapolis.

Russell began his dance career immediately after completing high school. He took a four-week training program at the franchised studio where he was going to work. This just whetted his appetite for dance, so he started taking lessons in different areas, including tap, ballet, and jazz. With his lessons completed, Russell began teaching in Chicago and worked with new students, giving them their first twenty lessons in ballroom dancing. He worked his way up the dance studio career ladder to become a supervisor. At this level, Russell trained all new students and was even training teachers. In this business, Russell points out, teachers need to be trained in interpersonal skills as well as in technical teaching skills, for they must help their students relax and overcome nervousness. It is also important for teachers to be able to explain in a clear way what the students need to do to accomplish their goals.

Teaching dance in a studio is definitely not a nine-to-five job. Most teachers work a sixty-hour week and spend at least two to three hours additionally every day working on their own dancing. Owning a dance studio franchise, as Russell has now done for many years, means even more work and responsibilities because you are running a small business. A franchise usually requires the services of a lawyer and a bookkeeper. The owner must keep records, collect fees, pay taxes, keep track of renewal dates, and follow local, state, and federal business and tax laws. In addition, obtaining a franchise and keeping the business going require developing a long-range plan.

Russell has been successful with his dance studio franchises. He believes that interest in dancing is growing and that people who are willing to devote enormous amounts of time and effort can have successful franchise operations.

A Teacher of Ballroom, Exercise Dancing, and Ballet

Johanna Bruyn is owner of Johanna's World of Dance. She was born in Indonesia and lived in the Netherlands before coming to the United States. As a child, she danced all the time. She had to abandon hopes for a dance career because of limited finances when her family moved to this country. Nevertheless, she never forgot her love of dance and always remembered the thrill she had turning and twirling as a young ballerina. Dance with all its joys came back into her life when she was twenty-seven and started going to discos. For three years, she drove to Chicago every weekend and trained with Charles and Rosemary Mattison. The Mattisons had impressive credentials as teachers, having won the prestigious Harvest Moon Ball dance contest. They used the prize money to open a studio to train others. Many of their students have also gone on to win the Harvest Moon Ball contest.

Johanna started teaching dance at the Free University in Indianapolis with Jim Skolburg. Their classes always had from sixty to eighty people at each session. The Free University was just getting started at this time, and the money made from the dance classes helped the university to become a viable school in the community. Johanna also started taking lessons from her next mentors, Dale Willman and Lee Harris. According to Johanna, lessons are always essential for dance teachers to keep their skills sharp and to pass on the latest steps to their students.

For almost six years Johanna operated her own studio; now she offers dance programs at clubs and community centers and as part of adult community education programs. She enjoys the flexibility of doing dance at different places. Johanna is such a successful teacher that she and her students have even danced the Viennese waltz in performance with the Indianapolis Symphony Orchestra.

Johanna also uses her background to teach a form of exercise workout she invented that uses jazz. Johanna likes a more stylized form of exercise than the usual aerobics. In her workout, there is more choreography and lots of stretches and isometrics. It is a low-impact form of exercise.

Johanna does not limit her teaching to her jazz workout or ballroom dancing. After she learned the art of teaching ballet from Virginia Holte, Johanna began teaching ballet; she now teaches more than one hundred little ballerinas. Her preschool classes have children from two and a half to five years old. Most ballet schools will not work with children this young. She gets all of her business from the word-of-mouth advertising of her satisfied students and a small ad in the yellow pages.

A Teacher of Social Dancing and Etiquette

Rebecca Kreuger Malenkos majored in English in college and became a high school English teacher, but her true love is dancing, which has always been a part of her life. She started taking dance lessons at the age of four and studied ballet, tap, jazz, and ballroom dancing for more than thirteen years. In high school, she not only danced but was also in the choir and musical productions. By the time Rebecca was in tenth grade, she had become a student assistant at the ballroom dancing school for young people where she had taken lessons in social dancing and etiquette since she was in sixth grade. She gained even more teaching experience in college through teaching ballroom dancing at Wake Forest University and at a neighboring women's college. Her six-week courses for college students were a way for the students not only to learn to dance but also to meet each other in a social situation. After college, Rebecca operated her own school in Texas called Rebecca's Cotillion, where she taught dance etiquette and such basic ballroom dances as the fox trot, waltz, swing, and tango. After moving to Indianapolis, she reopened Rebecca's Cotillion.

There is more than teaching dance to operating her school, Rebecca explains. Students have to receive written invitations, publicity must be done to advertise the school, and she has to solve the logistical problem of having an equal number of boys and girls for each class.

A College Professor of Dance

Stephan Laurent is the chair of the department of dance at Butler University and also an associate professor at the university. Like so many dance teachers, Stephan was a professional dancer with a long performance career before he started to teach. He didn't start studying dance until almost twenty, which is rather late for a professional dancer to begin.

Stephan interrupted his performance career to study at Southern Methodist University, where he received both his bachelor's and master's degrees. He became an associate professor of dance at the University of Wisconsin–Milwaukee, leaving there to become the artistic director of the Des Moines Ballet, now known as Ballet Iowa. Stephan then chose to move to Butler University, where 45 percent of the school's dance graduates go on to have a professional performing career—one of the highest number of graduates in the country to go into professional careers. In his present job, Stephan supervises the dance faculty, establishes the curriculum, and choreographs productions. Because the Butler Ballet Company is run like a professional company and puts on five or six shows a year, there is considerable choreographing for all the faculty members to do. Students also get a chance to choreograph, though the dance company is run by the faculty. Stephan explains that jobs like his at the university level require incredible dedication, energy, and physical, mental, and emotional endurance. They also allow dance lovers to be closely involved with several aspects of dancing.

Organizations for Dance Teachers

Dance lovers who are considering a career in the teaching of dance should contact dance associations for solid career information. Prospective dance teachers should also read the publications of these associations to keep abreast of what is happening in dance. And they should consider attending association conventions to meet dance teachers and watch demonstrations of the latest dance techniques.

The following dance organizations can provide helpful information to dance teachers.

Arthur Murray Dance Studios Organization
8303 Clairemont Mesa Boulevard
San Diego, CA 92111
www.sdarthurmurray.com

Artslynx International Arts Resources
www.artslynx.org/dance
> *This Internet resource provides links to a wide range of dance-related organizations and information about dance history, dance therapy, choreography, dancer health, employment, education, and notation.*

Chicago National Association of Dance Masters
5411 East State Street, Suite 202
Rockford, IL 61108
www.cnadm.com

Dance Educators of America
PO Box 607
Pelham, NY 10803
www.deadance.com

Dance Link
www.dancer.com/dance-links
  *Dance Link provides quick links to dance organizations and news
  groups worldwide.*

Dance Masters of America
PO Box 3458
Hickory, NC 28603
www.dma-national.org

Dance Vision International Dancers Association
ProDVIDA
9081 West Sahara Avenue
Las Vegas, NV 89117
www.prodvida.com

National Dance Council of America
PO Box 2816
Westfield, NJ 07090
www.ndca.org

National Dance Education Organization
4948 St. Elmo Avenue, Suite 301
Bethesda, MD 20814
www.ndeo.org

National Registry of Dance Educators
PO Box 254
Northport, NY 11768
www.nrde.org

United States Amateur Ballroom Dancers Association
PO Box 152998
Cape Coral, FL 33915
www.usabda.org

United States Imperial Society of Teachers of Dancing
316 Marina View Lane
Webster, NY 14580
www.usistd.org

Dance/Movement Therapy—Better Health Through Dancing

Dance/movement therapists use movement to improve the physical and emotional health of the people with whom they are working. The American Dance Therapy Association defines dance/movement therapy as the psychotherapeutic use of movement as a process that furthers the emotional and physical integration of the individual.

To become a dance/movement therapist, dance lovers need to complete both an undergraduate program with emphasis in psychology and training in a variety of dance forms, followed by professional training at the graduate level and an internship. You also need to be able to perform, choreograph, and teach dance. Dance/movement therapists need to have a strong desire to work with others and the patience, dedication, and stamina to get the job done.

The moving body is the medium of the dance/movement therapist's work. The therapist focuses on the communicative, expressive, and adaptive aspects of nonverbal behavior, using these to help clients effect changes in thinking, feeling, physical functioning, and behavior. The method consists of structuring and guiding bodily experience toward an expression of wholeness and self-awareness. This involves:

- identification and release of psycho-emotional-physical blocks in the body, thereby increasing range of motion
- increasing the dynamic range of the body's movement options or patterns
- providing a clear and safe context for the client to connect present bodily experience with past and present emotional traumas or issues
- facilitating a creative, imaginative, exploratory atmosphere where clients are able to discover and establish new patterns for interacting with others

According to the American Dance Therapy Association, dance/movement therapy is practiced in mental health rehabilitation programs, medical facilities, educational settings, nursing homes, day care centers, and disease-prevention and health-promotion programs. At the present time, these therapists must have a license to practice in most states as well as certification from the American Dance Therapy Association. The association distinguishes between therapists who are prepared to work within a team or under supervision and those who can work independently. Therapists with the title Dance Therapist Registered (DTR) have a master's degree and are fully qualified to work in a professional treatment system. Therapists with the title Academy of Dance Therapists Registered (ADTR) have met additional requirements and are fully qualified to teach, provide supervision, and engage in private practice. You can find general information about dance/movement therapy and information on the education required to be a therapist on the website of the association or by writing to:

American Dance Therapy Association
2000 Century Plaza, Suite 108
10632 Little Patuxent Parkway
Columbia, MD 21044
www.adta.org

Dance/movement therapists work with a variety of popula-
tions, including the emotionally disturbed or physically disabled,
children, adolescents, and older people. They work in both group
and individual sessions. They can also provide valuable information to a treatment team on a client's status and behavioral
patterns, make assessments, and propose movement-based inter-
ventions. Dance/movement therapy encourages the client to take
an active role in her or his own process of gaining or regaining
health and an optimal level of functioning.

A Dance/Movement Therapist

James Lobley is a registered dance/movement therapist (DTR). He
does both individual and group movement therapy in working
with children from the ages of three to twelve. James also does
family therapy through dance. The types of children with whom
he works include special needs children, developmentally delayed
children, children with social and emotional difficulties, and children who have been sexually abused. As a dance/movement therapist, he teaches social skills and helps children learn the proper
outlet for their feelings. Dance/movement therapy uses a holistic
approach in the way it perceives movement as an integral part of
the whole human being. Through physical movements, dance/
movement therapists are able to change people on a deeper psy-
chological level; they can also affect how clients perceive themselves. James has used fairy tales and creative movement to address
the developmental, personal, and interpersonal issues of children.

Career Path. In college, James majored in French and semiotics
at Brown University. After graduation, he danced for two years

while serving as an apprentice in woodworking. After a short while, he decided that he would rather work with people than inanimate objects, so he entered a two-year dance/movement therapy program at New York University. Few colleges in the United States have master's programs in dance/movement therapy. Becoming a registered dance/movement therapist is a long process that involves earning a master's degree plus completing a seven-hundred-hour internship. James did his internship at a private school for language-impaired children on Long Island. Returning to Indianapolis, he led movement recreational activities and gender and psychotherapy groups at a local hospital. He also has assisted in the development of treatment plans, offered individual counseling, and served as family liaison at a hospital.

Movement Analyst Specialist

As an assistant professor at Butler University, Idrienne Sobel-Steiman taught ballet dance to majors as well as dance therapists, fitness instructors, and other college students interested in understanding and changing movement of the body. Idrienne is a certified movement analyst. Most jobs for movement analysts are found in the college setting. Idrienne taught classes in body alignment, Laban movement analysis, and improvisation. In teaching these classes, she drew upon her background in three movement reeducation methods to teach the students techniques for changing poor or inefficient movement habits. She also used these techniques to teach them how to prevent injuries and strengthen their bodies. Idrienne worked mostly with ballet students. In the past twenty years, the process of teaching dance has become more anatomically and scientifically based as dancers want to learn more about movement. This has resulted in a demand for college teachers, like Idrienne, who can teach the science of dance.

Idrienne's educational background includes bachelor's and master's degrees in dance. She also has taken ballet lessons since she was eight, studying at such prestigious schools of dance as Juilliard and Joffrey and spending a summer at Le Centre de

Danse International in Cannes, France. In pursuing her original career choice of becoming a dancer, she worked with wonderful teachers like Andre Eglevsky from Russia, Melissa Hayden at Skidmore College, and her mentor, Marty Morginsky, who took her under his wing and helped and inspired her to develop her talent.

Career Path. Idrienne's career path includes jobs both in the dance and business worlds. After completing her bachelor's degree, Idrienne needed to find a job and got one in arts administration at the Joffrey Ballet. This was a full-time, forty-hour-a-week job, so she danced every evening in classes taught by Finis Jhung and David Howard. Idrienne's next career move was to decide she really wanted to teach and not dance in a company. To make sure this decision was right for her, she tried the business world, working on Wall Street in commodities and then at what she calls a great job with *Vogue* magazine, which didn't satisfy her because her heart remained with dancing.

After working in many different fields, she went to graduate school to get her master's in dance. During this time, she was teaching dance and dance workshops and working for physical therapists using her knowledge of therapeutic exercise, as well as seeing private patients. She was juggling a variety of jobs, including performing with the Joffrey company when it came to California, choreographing, and even performing as a movie extra. She also began to study with body therapists in the Los Angeles area and started to understand body therapies and the relationship of the mind and the body and how the mind affects movement. With this knowledge of dance and body movement, Idrienne knew she wanted to help people become more aware of themselves through movement, to help them get rid of pain through movement, and to enable them to function better in their lives whether they were dancers or secretaries or accountants. If Idrienne had to describe her career in the dance world, she would explain how she went from being a dancer who always wanted to perform to becoming an educator in a new field of dance.

More Information About Dance Careers

Dance is the most fundamental of the arts, as it gives people the opportunity to directly express themselves through their bodies. Not only is dance a powerful form of expression, it is a powerful medium for therapy. The job outlook is better for culture lovers looking for jobs with larger dance organizations than with small and midsize organizations that are having to cut back performances because of rising production costs. Opera companies and dance groups affiliated with colleges and universities and with television and motion pictures also offer some opportunities. With the general interest in dance increasing, the opportunities for employment in other areas aligned with dance have also increased.

Additional information about colleges and universities offering degrees in dance is available from:

National Dance Association (a Division of the American
Alliance for Health, Physical Education, Recreation, and
Dance)
1900 Association Drive
Reston, VA 20191
www.aahperd.ord/nda

The website of the National Association of Schools of Dance has a simple online version of its annual directory, which contains the names, addresses, and contact people for each accredited institution, community and precollegiate programs, nondegree-granting institutions, community or junior college, and degree-granting institutions offering programs and degrees. Or write to:

National Association of Schools of Dance (NASD)
11250 Roger Bacon Drive, Suite 21
Reston, VA 20190
http://nasd.arts-accredit.org

On the website of *Dance Magazine*, you can access a free database to identify programs that match your personal criteria for degree, type of dance, location, department size, tuition, and more. For more information, contact:

Dance Magazine
333 Seventh Avenue, Eleventh Floor
New York, NY 10001
www.dancemagazine.com

Other magazines that provide information about career opportunities in dance include:

Dance Teacher
Lifestyle Media
110 William Street, Twenty-Third Floor
New York, NY 10038
www.dance-teacher.com

Dance Spirit (also published by Lifestyle Media)
www.dancespirit.com

CHAPTER FIVE

Career Opportunities for Theater Lovers

Working Behind the Scenes of Theatrical Productions

The theater is so endlessly fascinating because it's so accidental.
It's so much like life.
—Arthur Miller, playwright

The word *theater* comes from the Greek word *theatron*, meaning a place for seeing. Theater, however, is far more than a building. It is a very complex art that requires many specialists to create a production. In the most sophisticated Broadway presentations, producers, directors, set designers, costume designers, lighting designers, sound designers, stagehands, and business staff are all needed to produce a play. In musical productions, choreographers, conductors, and orchestras are also required. In fact, all theatrical productions must have many people behind the stage. In small companies, many of the people involved handle more than one job or are volunteers gaining valuable career experience.

A theatrical performance is always an exciting event, whether it is on Broadway or in a small community theater. The attention of the audience is focused closely on the actors as the plot of a comedy, drama, or musical unfolds. At the end of the performance, the audience claps with approval of the production. It is not just the work of the actors that they are applauding. They are also applauding the work of all the theater lovers working backstage.

Where Theater Lovers Find Jobs

Not just in large cities but throughout the United States, groups are producing plays. Wherever plays are produced, there are jobs or opportunities to gain experience as unpaid volunteers. When theater lovers think of working in the theater, they may automatically think of jobs on Broadway, since it has achieved so much fame. There are, however, many other commercial (for-profit) theaters besides those on Broadway, although the latter generally require the largest staff. Off-Broadway theaters have smaller productions in smaller theaters with fewer staff people than on Broadway productions. Community theaters usually depend on volunteers, often with the exception of a paid director. Other opportunities for jobs in commercial theater exist in stock and dinner theaters, although stock productions usually only operate on a seasonal basis. Successful Broadway productions frequently spawn national touring companies that play in major cities like Chicago, Washington, and Los Angeles. Then smaller companies are formed to tour less populous areas. In addition, some companies mount theatrical productions for industrial shows.

More people are employed in nonprofit theater than in commercial theater. The greatest number of jobs is found in the theaters that are members of the League of Resident Theaters (LORT), a group of equity theaters including the American Conservatory Theater (ACT) in San Francisco, the Arena Stage in Washington, and the Actor's Theatre in Louisville, Kentucky. Other theaters in the nonprofit sector include off-off-Broadway theaters, theaters on college campuses, and children's companies.

Employment in off-off-Broadway theaters is usually for one play, and staff members receive very low wages. Some college theaters are professional theaters with a permanent staff, while most children's theaters are small and depend greatly on volunteers, unless they are members of LORT.

The Jobs Theater Lovers Want

There's no business like show business for theater lovers. They want to work in the same world that legends such as the Barrymores, Helen Hayes, Richard Burton, and Laurence Olivier once inhabited. Hollywood stars like Nicole Kidman, Natalie Portman, Julia Roberts, Christopher Walken, and Denzel Washington and television stars like Christina Applegate, John Goodman, and David Hyde Pierce have felt this magical attraction. It is not just the stars that attract theater lovers; it is the magic of seeing well-known plays such as *Death of a Salesman* and *A Streetcar Named Desire* performed live. In the first days of theater, there really weren't many jobs for theater lovers: the playwright did everything, including acting. Over the years, more specialists emerged to help performers bring plays to life. Here is a look at the behind-the-scenes jobs that you will find at a major repertory theater.

ARTISTIC
Artistic director
Director

PRODUCTION
Costume designer
Set designer
Lighting designer
Lighting crew
Sound designer
Sound technicians

Hair and makeup artists
Properties manager
Wardrobe attendants
Dressers
Stage manager
Stage staff
Construction crew

ADMINISTRATION
Development officer
Education director
Finance manager
Information technology specialist
Marketing manager
Public relations manager
Publications officer
Operations manager
Intern

What follows is a bird's-eye view of some jobs in the theater. In large companies there will be many jobs for assistants and interns, while in small companies each individual handles several jobs.

The Artistic Side of Theater

Directors

Directors are the interpreters of plays. They make the decisions that determine what the production as a whole will be like. This involves working with the designers of scenery, lighting, and costumes before and during the rehearsals so that each aspect of the play will reflect the planned mood or theme. Another area of responsibility for directors is selecting a cast that will give the desired performance. Directors also supervise the rehearsals and coordinate the work of everyone involved in the play to create the final product.

Directors may have collaborators, including assistant directors, stage managers, and secretaries. The stage managers are normally in charge of organizing tryouts and of coordinating backstage activity during performances. The route to becoming a director can often be traced back to having been a secretary, an assistant director, or a stage manager. Another path is through an internship as an assistant director. Most directors have learned this craft through studying in a theater program in college and graduate school.

Career Advancement and Earnings

The first work of fledgling directors is typically done while they are in college and is unpaid. Then they will usually work as directors of small productions for which they will receive a fee. It is not until directors have a body of twenty to thirty works that they are hired full-time. At this point, they may receive salaries in the low twenties. Because so many theatrical companies are small and only have one director, advancement in this profession usually occurs by moving to ever-larger companies.

The average earnings of salaried directors is around $46,000 a year. The lowest 10 percent earn less than $23,000 a year, while the highest 10 percent exceed $120,000. Summer theaters offer compensation, including royalties (based on the number of performances), usually ranging from $2,500 to $8,000 for a three- to four-week run.

The pay may be less at dinner theaters, but it has more potential for generating income through royalties. Regional theaters may hire directors for longer periods, thereby increasing their income. The highest-paid directors work on Broadway. While they commonly earn about $50,000 a show, a few top directors have become millionaires through their work as directors of highly successful productions.

From Artistic Director to Executive Director

The Indianapolis Civic Theatre is one of the ten largest community theaters in the United States. It is professionally staffed and has a budget of more than $1.6 million a year. Robert J. Sorbera is the executive director, which means that he is in charge of both the production and artistic staffs. For ten seasons, he was both the artistic director and the managing director, which is usually two jobs. The time required to handle both jobs was so great that Bob opted to become the executive director.

Artistic Director/Managing Director. In this dual position, Bob was responsible for both the artistic and business sides of the theater. As artistic director, Bob had the important responsibility of establishing the artistic philosophy of the theater and overseeing the quality of the productions. A big part of his job was selecting the plays performed in the theater. In addition, Bob would usually direct three or four plays each year, which required him to work at night five or six days a week during the six to ten weeks a play was in production. This job was made even more work intensive by his responsibilities on the business side as the managing director. In this role, Bob had the responsibility of overseeing operations, marketing, finance, development, and the education program.

Career Path. According to Bob, preparing to become a director is quite a complex undertaking. He believes that you need to have a certain amount of life experience in order to understand and handle the issues that you will be dealing with in plays. Also, because a director needs to be able to visualize what a play will look like, college course work in art and painting is important. In addition, there is the need to communicate your vision to set and lighting designers, which requires understanding not only the technical vocabulary but also what can be accomplished by these technicians. Since the 1950s, most directors have prepared for this career by studying how to direct in college. Bob earned a bachelor's degree in theater and his master's in directing. While in college, he directed a number of plays to qualify for his degree.

Like most college graduates who aspire to become directors, Bob found it difficult to get his first directing job. He began by doing a play here and there for free or just a $50 fee. These jobs helped him build a resume and led to his becoming the artistic director at a small theater outside of Green Bay, Wisconsin. After two years, Bob moved to the San Francisco Bay area, where he freelanced as a director with a number of companies. His next career step was to become a technical director at a children's theater, where he really learned the mechanics of putting on a production, from stage carpentry to sound to lighting. This enabled him to communicate effectively with technicians. After a short stint, again as a freelancer, Bob took a position as the artistic director of a community theater in Saginaw, Michigan. He remained there for eleven years before becoming artistic director/managing director and then executive director of the Indianapolis Civic Theatre.

Career Advice for Future Directors. Bob describes directing as a highly competitive job where only the best survive. It is also a career that requires long hours that last far into the night. In addition, it takes years to earn good wages in this field. Nevertheless, Bob encourages those who love directing to persevere in their goals because each day of their careers as directors will give them the artistic satisfaction they crave.

The Administrative Side of Theater

While most theater lovers may envision themselves working backstage, there are many jobs in the theater offices that must be done to keep a theater company functioning. Within this arena are the fund-raisers, accountants, box-office staff, publicists, marketing experts, educational program coordinators, group sales managers, and the clerical staff. And when a theatrical production goes on tour, a tour manager is needed to handle transportation and living quarters, oversee publicity and payroll, and deal with the presenters who are providing the facility for the play. In the commercial theater, a producer is needed to find the money for a play and hire the staff to produce it.

Director of Marketing

The responsibilities of marketing directors vary because of the different needs of theater companies. When James Habegger was director of marketing at the Indianapolis Civic Theatre, he was in charge of group sales, direct publicity, and advertising. He worked with a marketing team of four people to promote the theater to the public. They were the executive director of the theater, the director of marketing, the director of development, and the director of publicity. Teamwork was the key to his job. When James had a good radio or television spot and the director of development had a good corporate sponsor, they worked to bring these two elements together.

Career Path. James's college background is in performance arts and music. His interest in the theater can be traced back to high school and college performances in musicals. After graduation from college, James pursued his musical interests by performing at Bear Creek Farms, a one-hundred-seat theater, as part of a group that put on musical reviews. James's next job was at a dinner theater in North Carolina, where he performed in five shows a week and made $35 a show. To earn living expenses, he worked as a maintenance man in a hotel. After a year in show business, James went to work with an insurance company because he simply couldn't make enough money in the theater. His job consisted of answering angry phone calls eight hours a day, which he feels was good training for working with the public as a director of marketing. James had just started taking marketing classes when he obtained his job at the Civic Theatre. At night, this theater lover would perform in musicals at another theater, since returning to his own theater would be like going back to work.

Director of Development

Directors of development are fund-raisers. When Kathy Daniels held this position at the Civic Theatre before leaving to work for a foundation, she raised money for the theater from individuals, corporations, and governmental entities. Part of her job consisted of cultivating an awareness with potential donors of what the Civic Theatre was, what it did, and how their donations would benefit the community and the theater.

Approximately half of Kathy's time on the job was devoted to securing and writing grants. Every year, she applied for more than twenty grants. She had to meet the deadline for each grant and fulfill the different requirements every grant had. A part-time assistant helped her accomplish these tasks. Another part of her job was developing brochures for the annual campaigns directed at individuals and corporations. Not only did she develop the brochures for these campaigns, she also created the database of potential donors. In addition, Kathy developed packets that highlighted the benefits of corporate sponsorship to the companies and to the community. The sponsoring company's logo was then placed on all ads. To build ongoing relationships with the sponsors, she kept them up-to-date with what was happening at the theater and gave them copies of press releases and ads and some free tickets. It was also necessary for her to keep track of all money that she was able to raise and to send acknowledgments to all donors thanking them for their gifts or sponsorships.

Job Requirements. Being a director of development at the Civic Theatre is a real hands-on job. Kathy answered her own phone calls and spent a lot of time on the computer typing and creating materials. Even though Kathy had not completed a degree in arts administration, which lets future development directors specialize in the areas of fund-raising and public relations, she had taken many continuing education courses sponsored by the National Society for Fund Raising Executives and courses at the Indiana University Center on Philanthropy. She took courses on annual campaigns, planned giving, major gifts, capital campaigns, and grant writing and found them very helpful. To succeed in a job in development, Kathy believes that you must like people and be excited about and believe in the product you are selling, just as she believed in the productions and programs of the Civic Theatre. Then, it is much easier to ask people for money.

Director of Education

Civic theaters are especially interested in helping children gain acting skills as well as learn more about theater. As director of education at the Indianapolis Civic Theatre, Brent Marty is in charge of administering the theater's education program for both children and adults. At the present time, the theater offers the following programs:

- **Workshops for children:** storytelling for preschoolers, some scripted productions for elementary school children, scripted productions for seventh graders, and staged productions including musical theater
- **Adult education program** for beginners to advanced, with classes in dance, yoga, singing, pilates, and music theater
- **Student matinees** for schoolchildren at the theater
- **Student productions** for ages six to fourteen and fourteen to twenty-one that are run like normal theatrical productions, giving participants the opportunity to work with professionals

In order to administer all of these programs, Brent has to hire teachers, develop the curriculum, and market the program. All this is done in close collaboration with others at the theater. Brent also has a part-time assistant who handles student enrollment, fields phone calls, and assists him as needed.

Career Path. Brent got bit by the theater bug early. At five, he was Santa Claus in a school play. He was also fortunate that his family supported his interest. His grandmother frequently took him to the theater. In high school, he was active in the theater; he was also in the choir and orchestra. Originally, he started college as a music major with a business minor but switched to a theater major as a sophomore. During college, he performed in many theatrical productions, worked backstage, and did some musical direction. After college, Brent wasn't really sure what he wanted to do. He tried working on the West Coast and discovered that wasn't where he wanted to be. Then he moved to Chicago, where he did temp work and got occasional theater jobs. During college, Brent's mentor had told him that he should be a teacher. He returned home to Indianapolis and found a job in a high school as an aid and accompanist in the music department. At the same time, he was working at the Civic Theatre as a musical director for some productions where he had a show-by-show contract. Then he started teaching for them. When the position of director of education opened up, he applied for and was offered his present job. Brent still acts whenever he can at other theaters and also serves as music director for most Civic Theatre productions.

Career Advice. Brent notes that more universities are now offering degrees in arts administration. He believes that this degree is excellent preparation for careers with theater companies as most are too small to have career ladders.

Volunteer Coordinator

Adrienne Reiswerg grew up in New York City, close to Broadway. She went to many shows with her family and developed a love of the theater when she was quite young. Adrienne has continued this family tradition by taking her sons to the theater in Indianapolis. In school, camp, and college, she was involved in dramatics. Adrienne's college training was in education, and she taught elementary school for five years. On returning to the work arena after starting a family, she obtained a job working for the Riley Hospital Telethon as a volunteer coordinator. The job of recruiting volunteers and designing volunteer projects had flexible work hours, involved some travel, and gave her the opportunity to work with different groups. She left this job to enjoy raising her family, acting in community theater, and serving as a volunteer at the Civic Theatre.

While Adrienne was a volunteer, money became available at the Civic Theatre to hire a person to match interested volunteers with programs needing personnel, to expand the volunteer program, and to create new projects. The sum available for this position was only sufficient to fund a part-time job, which was ideal for Adrienne. For several years she worked nineteen hours a week as the volunteer coordinator, with some weekend and evening hours. This position no longer exists at the Civic Theatre; however, other theaters do have volunteer coordinators or people who handle this responsibility.

Adrienne got her job through her activities as a volunteer because she was in the right place at the right time and because she was able to accept part-time work. Prerequisites for this job include the ability to speak in public, write clearly, and organize and execute projects. In this field, you should also like to work with people. While a theater or college degree is not essential for her job, most theater companies tend to hire individuals with degrees.

Adrienne enjoyed her job because she worked with wonderful people while making a contribution to the theater. She also found it satisfying to know that she was part of an organization that brings beauty and recreation to so many—in addition to being thought provoking.

Because Adrienne was only a part-time employee, her benefits were not the same as those of full-time employees with health and insurance benefits. However, she enjoyed the benefits of flexible hours. And believe it or not, this theater lover spent part of her free time doing volunteer work at other theaters.

The Production Side of Theater

Costume Designer

Clare Gee became interested in theater during high school. Because her school was small, she became involved in every aspect of the theater when she participated in plays—from acting to set building. She planned to major in English and minor in theater at college. However, after two years of college, she changed her major to science and became a science teacher.

Working as a freelance seamstress gave Clare the opportunity to learn sewing techniques. Her introduction to the world of costume design came when she volunteered to sew for a theater. Through this activity, she learned costuming skills that she put to work with her theater background. Then she became a freelance costume designer, making costumes for local theaters. The next step was a position as costume supervisor at the Christian Repertory Theater, where she worked four or five hours a day and enjoyed a flexible schedule. After making costumes for one show at the theater, she was asked to organize and operate the costume shop.

Clare uses her educational background, especially her history courses, when she is doing research to determine what type of costumes would be appropriate for a play. She especially enjoys the study and research and then moving on to a new and different project. She picked up her sewing skills through personal practice and has taken art courses to improve her sketching.

As Clare has demonstrated, it is not difficult to get into the costume design department at a community theater as a volunteer.

However, to be paid for this work you must demonstrate that you are efficient, can be creative with the allotted budget, and produce good design work.

Set Designer

Sets aren't just pretty backgrounds for theatrical productions. They are the environment where the action takes place. Sets add to actors' characterizations as well. If the curtain goes up on a messy room with papers all over the floor, you get a different impression of the character who lives in this room than if the room were absolutely spotless. Sets also tell the audience about the time and place a play is portraying—such as colonial or Victorian, in New England or in Mexico. Audiences can also expect the set to define the mood of a play. Successful sets increase an audience's understanding of a play.

For several years, Joel Fontaine was resident set designer for American Conservatory Theatre (ACT) in San Francisco. This was an unusual job since most set designers are freelancers. Joel's work in designing the set for a play begins when he reads the play a couple of months before rehearsals for the play are to start. If he were freelancing, Joel would also visit the theater at this time so he could make his design fit the theater. After reading the play, the next step for set designers is a meeting with the director to discuss what the play means. Joel may bring pictures to this meeting to show what he thinks the look or the mood of the play is. If Joel and the director have worked together previously, the first meetings are smoother. At the next meeting with the director, Joel presents rough sketches or a model. The director's reaction can range from loving to hating Joel's initial ideas. However, over the course of three or more meetings with the director, Joel refines his sketches until the two have agreed on a working model that is done to scale.

At this point, the producer of the play may also be consulted for his or her approval. Joel then makes a finished model—with every detail complete, from paint to furniture to molding on the door. A few designers have help from assistants in constructing the finished model. Joel then shows the director the completed model as a final step in the design process.

Joel did not draw the construction details when he worked at ACT. Instead, an ACT shop draftsperson would do this. While the set was being built at the ACT shop, Joel might check on it. Once a set was built, it went to the paint shop. At times, Joel had to give the scene painter a flat rendering of the set if the painting was to be quite complex. While the set was being built, Joel had to confer with the lighting, prop, and costume designers. He wanted to make sure that all of these elements would blend with his design. He certainly didn't want an actor to be wearing a plaid outfit in the same design as the upholstery on the couch.

When he freelances, Joel may draw the construction details, paint the set, and get the props. Joel goes to a play rehearsal and shows the actors the model of the set and checks at this time to ensure that the actors aren't walking through places on the stage that will be walls.

Approximately a week to ten days before the play opens, the scenery is taken to the theater. Now is the time the set designer checks that everything works as it should. The lighting and sound designers now come to work on the set. Joel remains at the technical rehearsal while all the lighting and sound problems are solved. The actors wear their costumes at the dress rehearsal, and changes are made so everything works together—scenery, lighting, costumes, and paint.

Career Path. Joel began his career in New York City assisting other designers and doing design work himself, after completing a master's program in set design at Yale. Joel is a set designer in the theater simply because he can't imagine doing anything else. The two major frustrations of his career as a freelancer are low wages and always having to be looking for his next job.

Design Associate

At the ACT, Joel had a design associate, Dawn Swiderski, who also freelanced and did shows at other theaters. She did many of the tasks Joel would have to do when he freelanced. When Joel completed the set design, she did the construction drawings for the scene shop. She then served as the liaison between the set designer and the shop. She also had to work closely with the scene painter. At all times, she had to make sure that everyone in the carpentry shop and paint shop had all the necessary information. Dawn was already familiar with set design before she came to the ACT, as she had assisted professional set designers when she was in college studying for her bachelor's degree in theater design and production. After college, she got a design internship at ACT and became an associate designer when her predecessor left.

After four years with ACT, Dawn left the theatrical realm for a career in films. Her first job was as a set designer for *James and the Giant Peach*. In film work, a set designer's job is primarily making working drawings and models. Dawn became an assistant art director, which involved supervising the work of set designers. The next step up the ladder for her was to become the art director of a film. When Dawn worked on a movie, she worked twelve-hour days. She worked through a union that sets a base price for her work, and then Dawn negotiated her own deals. Set designers are paid on an hourly basis, while assistant art directors are paid weekly.

Set Builder

After the designer and the director have agreed on the design of a set, the designer or an assistant makes a detailed set of drawings that shows every detail of the construction. Large theater organizations have their own shops or use independent firms that specialize in building sets. In the case of nonprofessional companies, the set designer and a volunteer crew may do all the construction using the stage as their shop. ACT has its own shop, which also builds sets for other stage shows in San Francisco and throughout the country.

Before Ed Raymond became the union representative for the stagehands union, he was the scene shop foreman of the ACT scene shop and the technical supervisor of the ACT company. As shop foreman, he supervised a core crew of four or five plus a scene painter. Depending on the time allotted for a job, the complexity of the set design, and the money available, Ed's crew could expand to as many as twenty people. Everyone working on the crew, including Ed, was a member of the union. When Ed needed to hire additional crew, he hired union people who could do the job. The union has an apprentice stagehand program to train stagehands for working in the theater, movies, and television. Apprentices gain experience through scene shop work, lectures, and reading material for self-study. In addition to the union crew, Ed usually had two interns just out of college, working for a very small amount of money to get exposure to set building and designing.

There was not much turnover in Ed's crew because they truly enjoyed this work. Job seekers who get crew jobs usually have had experience building scenery in college or elsewhere. It must be pointed out that these jobs, including Ed's, are seasonal. The crew only works when there is a job to do. For Ed, this usually meant approximately eight months a year. Only a few scene shops employ crews full-time.

In his role as shop foreman, Ed often found himself covered with sawdust as he worked with his crew to build the set. They frequently had to consult the blueprints to make sure the set was being built precisely as the set designer envisioned. The designer consulted with Ed during the design process to ensure that the ideas could be built within the budget allowed and that the set as designed could be constructed as a light and portable unit. Ed's job as shop foreman included deciding which materials would be needed for each job and then ordering them. He also had to make sure that all of the work was done within the limits of the budget. In addition to building the set, Ed's crew was responsible for constructing all the mechanical effects—the elevators, cranes, and winches—used in a show.

When a set was built, Ed's job as technical supervisor began. In that capacity, he coordinated taking the set to the theater with other performance and rehearsal schedules. While at the theater, as well as in the shop, he worked directly under the production manager. He would stay on the set during rehearsal to make sure everything about the set was functioning as planned. When the production had finished its run, Ed was in charge of removing the set. Since each set is unique, few sets are stored. Instead, only the recyclable elements are saved.

Career Path. Ed never planned to work at building scenery, even though he possessed considerable skills developed from using the excellent shop in his family's home. He graduated from college with a degree in English literature and taught in elementary school, high school, and college for a while. Then a friend who was an assistant foreman in the shop at ACT told Ed about his work, and Ed was intrigued enough with the job description to start as a shop general, the lowest position in the shop. His job was basically to keep the shop clean.

Ed then became a shop mechanic. This is the job title for those who read the blueprints and assemble the sets. After a stint as assistant foreman, Ed changed his job milieu and went to work as an assistant stage carpenter. In this job, he was responsible for putting up the set when it was delivered to the theater. At this particular theater, he might have to put up the sets for two shows in one day. This was a full-time job, working seventy-five- to eighty-hour weeks. He also toured with ACT as a property master in charge of the show's props. Then he returned to the ACT scene shop as foreman. When Ed was not working at ACT, he worked for a film company, LucasArts, as a foreman and as a construction coordinator. This job was very similar to what he did at ACT except that the sets, crews, and budgets were bigger.

Lighting Designer

As a freelance lighting designer, Derek Duarte is in charge of all the lighting for a play or theatrical production. He must organize the technical elements as well as the artistic design. His job starts at the beginning of rehearsals and lasts to opening night, when an electrician takes over running the lights for the actual performances. By the time the curtain goes up on opening night, all the instructions for running the lights have been put in the computer.

Derek starts his work with four bare walls—a blank canvas on which to create all the lighting effects. For example, if the director says that a scene will take place on a stormy, hot night, Derek has to create this night with the lighting designs he selects. Like the set and costume designers, he must read the play and meet with the director, as well as the other designers. Set designers and costume designers can make drawings or have fittings before the start of rehearsals, but it is a different story for lighting designers, who can make schematic drawings but cannot really put the finishing touches on their work until load-in time. This is the time when everything is brought to the theater and rehearsals on the stage begin. During this time, Derek puts in extended hours, working six days a week, from eight in the morning until midnight. Eighty percent of lighting designers' work is preproduction planning. The rest of their work is done after the scenery arrives. Being a lighting designer is an exciting, high-pressure job, but Derek finds it fascinating each time he sees what he has created.

Derek has known since he was sixteen years old that he wanted to work in the theater. He always knew that he did not want to be on the stage as a performer, so he looked through a theater program for all the jobs listed for a theatrical production; he decided that being a lighting designer was the job for him. After attending a community college, he got his bachelor's degree in dramatic arts from the University of California at Berkeley. While he was at the community college, he participated in a work study program, getting minimum wage for being a stagehand. In college he worked at the renowned Berkeley Repertory Theater, a wonderful experience because the performers were from around the world. Derek obtained a master's degree in fine arts in lighting design from the University of California at Los Angeles. During his graduate studies, he was a teaching assistant and ran a lab on constructing scenery. All of Derek's jobs during his college days augmented his classroom instruction while paying for his schooling.

Career Path. After graduation, Derek took numerous small jobs in the performing arts. He really never settled anywhere, but instead traveled from job to job, living in New York, San Francisco, and Los Angeles. There is considerable travel involved in being a costume, set, or lighting designer, as you have to go to where the jobs are. Derek has even traveled to Hong Kong to do a show. Returning to the San Francisco Bay Area, Derek took a job teaching lighting design for one year at the University of California–Berkeley, replacing someone on sabbatical. Since then he has kept the Bay Area as his home and worked for community theaters around the country. Today, besides being a lighting designer, he teaches several theater classes at the University of Santa Clara. In his free time, just like every other theater lover, Derek enjoys going to the theater; however, it usually takes him ten minutes to relax and settle in to enjoy the show. During those first ten minutes, he is busy checking out the set's scenery and lighting.

Sound Designer

Sound designers produce the program sound, which includes both sound effects and sound reinforcement. To make the ideal contribution to the production, the sound designer has to make the sound an integrated part of the production. Sound includes music, noises of no recognizable origin, realistic sounds such as doorbells and thunder, and any sound that is mechanically produced. In the theater, sounds that are produced electrically are considered to be part of the stage lighting.

The sound designer helps set the play's mood and enhance the story through sounds such as gunshots, offstage screams, and screeching brakes. Sounds can either be live and created for each production or prerecorded. The sound designer holds the same type of discussions with the director as the costume, set, and light designers do, only this time the discussion is about what should be heard during the play. Sound designers select sounds and play them to the director for approval. Once the sounds have been approved, the sound designer makes a list of the equipment to be used and where it is to be placed. Like the lighting director, much of the work is done after the load-in. The sound director is also concerned with enhancing the sound of the actors and the orchestra, if there is one.

Important Facts About Theater Jobs

Individuals considering a career working behind the scenes in the theater should realize that jobs in the performing arts are not usually permanent, except for jobs of an administrative or clerical nature. Jobs such as director and costume, set, and lighting designers usually begin and end with a show, unless one is working for a LORT theater. People take jobs in the theater because they love the surroundings. Many individuals working in the theater also hold outside jobs to earn more money because jobs in the theater do not offer high wages or job security. As you read earlier in the chapter, besides freelancing as a lighting designer, Derek Duarte is also teaching at a university. He tells his theater students that most of them will be working at another job but will find every moment they work in the theater a joy.

A Look at Several Part-Time Jobs

The San Jose Repertory Theatre is a regional theater located in the heart of downtown San Jose. It presents innovative productions of the classics, combined with daring contemporary works, and has a commitment to developing new plays. The theater has made a significant contribution to the community through its imaginative education and outreach programs. The following part-time job openings at the theater provide a good idea of the qualifications regional theaters expect job seekers to possess.

Part-time IT consultant for proprietary software. The Rep has recently acquired the newest CRM database for the arts: Tessitura. This software provides a comprehensive suite of ticketing, marketing, development, and fund-raising tools to share information, increase productivity, and provide unparalleled leverage for customer relationship management. Tessitura uses Microsoft SQL Server 2000 Standard or Enterprise edition with appropriate SQL Server client licenses for all workstations.

The Rep is looking to hire someone for a part-time position (eight to sixteen hours a week) that requires database administration skills as well as SQL report writing; experience with Tessitura is a plus. Great interpersonal skills are a must.

The primary responsibilities include creating custom reports from database using Sybase's InfoMaker and maintaining the database (back-up and job schedule and performing upgrades to software).

Customer Service Agent. The theater is seeking applicants for a part-time position (twenty hours per week) to work in the box office for the season. Duties include processing ticket orders via phone, e-mail, and fax; preparing box office for show days (printing will-call notices); responding to patron issues; and providing the highest level of customer service.

Skills and qualification required include experience using Microsoft Excel, Word, and Outlook. Must be highly organized with strong attention to detail and able to multitask. Must be able to work under pressure in a fast-paced and fun environment. Applicants should possess excellent communication skills, both verbal and written.

Inside Sales Associate. Inside Sales Department looking for self-motivated, artistic, and effective salespeople to promote the theater season. Great part-time job, twenty to thirty hours a week.

Production Positions. The Rep is continually accepting resumes from interested individuals to add to our overhire lists in the costume, scene, prop, and electric departments. Skilled individuals are called as needed for continual load-ins, focus, strikes, and large builds.

Public Relations Intern. Seeking public relations, marketing, and theatre interns to aid in creating and implementing public relations programs for San Jose Repertory Theatre. Working directly with the associate director of communications, the intern will assist in writing press materials, clerical work, event management, and other duties as assigned. Position offers the opportunity to learn public relations skills and enhance writing and research skills. Candidates will also be proficient in MS Office and be able to perform Internet research. The hours are flexible, but you will need to commit to two days per week. Our internships are unpaid but can be used for school credit.

Website/Marketing Research Intern. Seeking public relations, marketing, and theatre interns to aid in creating and implementing website programs for San Jose Repertory Theatre. Working directly with the associate director of communications, the intern will conduct photo and history research on the Rep's past and current productions; assist in writing website materials, and perform other tasks as assigned. Position will offer the opportunity to enhance writing and research skills.

Searching for a Job in the Theater

Many people currently working in the theater found their first jobs after working as interns or volunteers. Networking is another way to find out about jobs. In addition, the following newspapers and periodicals provide job information for theater lovers.

Newspapers

Billboard
770 Broadway
New York, NY 10003
www.billboard.com
   (music entertainment industry)

Variety
5700 Wilshire Boulevard, Suite 120
Los Angeles, CA 90036
or
360 Park Avenue South
New York, NY 10010
www.variety.com
   (entertainment news, media jobs)

Magazines

Live Design
249 West Seventeenth Street
New York, NY 10011
www.livedesignonline.com
> (*lighting, staging, and projection for live entertainment professionals*)

Stage Directions
Lifestyle Media
110 William Street, Twenty-Third Floor
New York, NY 10038
www.stage-directions.com
> (*strategic, practical, and technical information needs of small theaters*)

CHAPTER SIX

More Career Opportunities for Culture Lovers

Working with Other Fine Arts

Men are so inclined to content themselves with what is commonest;
the spirit and the senses so easily grow dead to the impressions of
the beautiful and perfect . . . . For this reason, one ought every day
at least, to hear a little song, read a good poem, see a fine picture,
and if it were possible, to speak a few reasonable words.
—Goethe, *Wilhelm Meister's Apprenticeship*

If you have the opportunity to work in a career where you are supporting the arts, your career satisfaction is likely to be high. While some may think that such a career for a culture lover only involves art, music, dance, and the theater, this is a rather narrow view. The arts world also includes literature, architecture, photography, furniture, textiles, and jewelry. As the list of arts expands, so does the list of possible jobs for culture lovers. There are certainly jobs in museums, galleries, corporations, and stores for culture lovers with these less-traditional interests. The list of possible jobs increases further when you consider all the jobs that deal with more than one art form. Government agencies, foundations, and concert halls offer enticing opportunities for culture lovers who want to work with several art forms.

Be creative in searching for your perfect job in the arts. It is so easy to surf on the Net for all the job possibilities. Visit the websites of museums, symphony orchestras, theaters, and foundations, and you will see the wide range of jobs available for culture lovers who want a career associated in some way with the arts. Don't shun the lowest job on the career ladder in your field of interest, since it will acquaint you with the existence of more jobs in this area than you probably ever imagined. And remember that many of the culture lovers in this book found jobs by serving as interns or volunteers. Culture lovers should also search for jobs by such traditional routes as newspaper and magazine ads; school placement offices; city, state, and federal employment offices; and private employment agencies. Here are just a few more places where art lovers can find jobs.

Unique Stores for Culture Lovers

There are stores that specialize in the selling of fine arts objects and very elegant objects for the home. Some of these stores are world famous, like Gump's in San Francisco. These stores do not just exist in metropolitan areas. Within many communities there are stores that seem almost like museums—places in which to browse rather than to shop. They are intriguing places for culture lovers to work, especially if they are interested in several forms of arts. Culture lovers may find it especially appealing to work as salespersons and buyers in these stores.

Working at a Very Special Store

For many years, Ron Schwarz worked at Gump's, where his office was a culture lover's delight. Oriental scrolls hung on the walls, and sculpture abounded. Nevertheless, his desk was stacked with papers attesting to the fact that there was considerable paperwork in his dual role as divisional merchandise manager for the third floor and director of interior design. As part of these jobs, he bought all the lamps, furniture, and Asian art sold in the store.

This involved seeing sales representatives in his office, going to shows and furniture markets, and traveling to such cities as New York, Paris, and Milan. These buying trips were not artistic flings, since he had a budget that limited what he could purchase. An important job requirement for buyers is to have a strong business sense. In addition, Ron points out that successful buyers must go beyond their personal tastes and choose items that would appeal to the commercial market.

Ron's jobs carried many responsibilities. He helped create the room settings on the third floor and supervised the look of the floor. He coordinated the colors used in the store. He supervised personnel and hired new sales associates and interior designers. For both of these positions, he was more inclined to look at a job seeker's background than at the academic degrees. Because of the uniqueness of Gump's furnishings, clients from around the world seek the services of the design staff. Ron spent part of his time matching the clients to the appropriate designers.

Ron has both a background in art and experience in the retail and design worlds. Although he majored in art in college, he believes that his knowledge of the arts with which he deals comes mainly from constant reading, studying, looking, and visiting museums. Culture lovers aspiring to positions like the one Ron had with Gump's must share this attribute of always wanting to know more. In addition, a background of varied experiences is helpful.

Career Path. After the army, Ron's first job was designing a line of furniture for an importer, followed by a job working for an antiques dealer, and then briefly owning his own interior design studio. A part-time Christmas sales job at Tiffany's led to a position as an assistant glass buyer in only six months and later to actually designing and buying china. In 1966, Ron opened his own store in San Francisco, where he sold such objects as china, glass, and silver and worked as an interior designer doing primarily residential work. After he closed his store to concentrate on interior design, he was asked to work at Gump's, which let him use all of his prior experiences. When Gump's discontinued the furniture and interior design departments after moving to a new location, Ron returned to his career as an interior designer. Today, he helps clients put together collections of antiques, which involves educating and consulting with them as well as finding fine arts objects for them. As Ron has clients throughout the United States and the world seeking his expertise, so his job involves considerable travel. It gives him an opportunity to shop throughout the world.

Antiques Shops—Dealing in Valuable Art Objects

Many people tend to think of antiques as old household articles; however, other objects should be included in this category, such as coins, books, guns, toys, and even clothing. It isn't just age, however, that makes an object an antique. It can be valued for the skill of its craftsman or because it is rare. Lovers of antiques can find jobs working with antiques as shop owners, salespersons, appraisers, auctioneers, restorers, and repairers. And there is no shortage of antiques shops in which antiques lovers can work. Large cities have hundreds of shops, and even the smallest community may have a shop or two, especially if the area attracts tourists.

Owning an Antiques Shop

For many antiques lovers, a lifelong dream is to have their own shop to sell their favorite types of antiques. You can find shops specializing in ancient Chinese porcelains and accessories, seventeenth-century French furniture, nautical antiques, brass lamps, or whatever antiques shop owners fancy. John Drum owns his own antiques shop specializing in eighteenth- and nineteenth-century decorative furniture. He employs two salespeople. When hiring employees, John looks for people who know the basic facts about antiques and are super salespeople. He believes that successful antiques dealers not only must have an eye for what will sell but must also have good business skills.

John learned about antiques by growing up in a home furnished with eighteenth-century English and French furniture and other antiques his family had inherited. He studied marketing in college and worked in business for several years. After the death of his father, he decided to set up a very small antiques shop with the possessions he had inherited. Before he opened the shop, he took a three-month course in London at the Study Center for the Decorative Arts. Subsequently, John learned about buying antiques when he went to Europe with a friend who taught him how to restock his shop.

Today, John makes two trips to Europe a year, mostly to France. Over the years, he has established a network of shops to visit, but John is always trying to find new shops. Trips abroad are not restful. Days are often twelve to fourteen hours long and distances covered can be great. On one trip, he covered three thousand kilometers in five days. He may just double-park in front of a shop and run in to see if they have anything he is looking for. John also shops locally and attends auctions to restock his shop. Restocking an antiques shop is a major job for every antiques dealer.

Besides restocking his shop, John handles many other tasks. He must spend time in his shop, selling antiques and seeing that the antiques he has purchased are repaired or restored if necessary. He usually hires others to do repair and restoration work. Time must also be spent visiting other shops and studying catalogs in order to price his antiques appropriately. Before new articles can go on the sales floor, he must write up a description of the article for the sales tag and price the piece. In addition, like most other antiques shop owners, he takes furniture to shows to sell it.

Books as Works of Art

In the middle ages, monks would sit at their desks in monasteries painstakingly copying books that were truly beautiful to behold. Today, there are calligraphers, papermakers, printmakers, typographers, bookbinders, and printers making books in artistic ways.

These publishers often combine literature and art in a fine arts manner. A few just print visual art with text. The materials published by these companies do not have mass appeal. They are rarely sold in bookstores, except in rare and antiquarian stores.

There are no large publishers printing these books. Some are just individuals with tabletop presses wishing to make outstanding books of a grandmother's poetry or a buddy's Vietnam War experiences. Others are print shops with five or six employees. Only a few fine-print publishers make money; most are just self-supporting.

Libraries and colleges often have book arts programs where people can learn printing, typography, and other skills essential to publishing. More information about this field can be obtained by writing to:

Guild of Book Workers
521 Fifth Avenue
New York, NY 10175
http://palimpsest.stanford.edu/byorg/gbw

The Guild was founded to "establish and maintain a feeling of kinship and mutual interest among workers in the several hand book crafts." On its website, the Guild has a resource list for those seeking instruction in the book arts.

Publishing Companies

Book lovers can be actively involved in the publishing of literary works at many publishing companies. Acquisitions editors read hundreds of manuscripts and work with literary agents to find new books to publish. Editors work closely with the authors of fine literature in the preparation of their manuscripts once they've been selected for publication. Publishing professionals in administration and marketing handle the advertising, promotion, sales, and distribution end of publishing.

Antiquarian and Rare Bookstores

Book lovers do not have to print their own books to be associated with extraordinary books. A few bookstores just deal in antiquarian and rare books, giving book lovers the opportunity to own or work in a store buying or selling these literary treasures.

Performing Arts Centers

For the culture lovers who wish to be involved with opera companies, symphony orchestras, ballet companies, and theater and choral groups, working as part of the staff at a performing arts center provides this opportunity. The size of the hall greatly determines the size and functions of the staff. The three largest performing arts centers are Lincoln Center in New York City, the Los Angeles Music Center, and the Kennedy Center in Washington, D.C. These centers have large permanent staffs with dozens of administrative and technical positions, as do many large universities with performing arts centers. Community performing arts centers, on the other hand, may be operated entirely by volunteers. However, these centers are excellent places for volunteers to get the experience that may lead to a full-time, paid position with a larger center.

On the Staff at Clowes Hall

On the campus of Butler University, Clowes Hall is one place in Indianapolis where opera, ballet, musical, and theatrical productions are presented. While Clowes Hall is decidedly not as large as the three largest performing arts centers, it does have opportunities for a variety of staff jobs in these areas:

ADMINISTRATION
Executive director
Director of administrative services
Director of production

EDUCATION
Education manager
Education coordinator and distance learning

MARKETING AND COMMUNITY RELATIONS
Marketing and promotions manager
Technology and communications coordinator/webmaster
Public relations and sponsorship manager

BOX OFFICE
Ticket manager
Sales staff

STAGE PRODUCTION
Carpenter/foreman
First electrician/lights
Second electrician/sound
Stage technician/flyman
Stage technician/video-DL

FRONT-OF-HOUSE OPERATIONS
Receptionist
House manager

SERVICE
Lead custodian
Custodian

. . . .

Architectural Showplaces

There are places that have such interesting architecture that they literally take your breath away. It is a treat to stand in these buildings and view their design, the innovative use of materials, and the creative genius of the architect. If you visit these places—such as the Vanderbilt House in New York City, designed by George B.

Post; Taliesen, the Wisconsin home of Frank Lloyd Wright; the Lincoln Memorial; or the Kennedy Center for Performing Arts—you have the opportunity to see architectural masterpieces. At the same time, there are opportunities for employment in these places that should be very appealing to those who are lovers of architecture and interior design. Employees are needed to handle the day-to-day operation of these places, which includes taking charge of administrative tasks, from personnel to finance to public relations; operating gift shops; coordinating volunteers and docents; soliciting funds; renting the space for events; and running an education program. While some architectural landmarks may not have any paid employees, several have quite large staffs. Quite often, people who work in these places have first served as interns or volunteers.

Manager of Meetings and Events Marketing

One of the outstanding examples of modern architecture in California is the San Francisco Museum of Modern Art. It has a dramatic atrium space that is surrounded by four floors of galleries. Hillary Adams worked within this magnificent setting as the manager of meetings and events marketing. It was Hillary's job to market the space of the museum to groups for parties and meetings and to ensure that each event held at the museum was a success. She found it easy to market the space, as the museum is within easy walking distance of the convention center and major hotels. Instead of contacting individual corporations and conventions that might wish to use the space after the museum closes, she focused on working with meeting planners at the visitors bureau and local-destination management companies, as these organizations know who is looking for space for events.

Hillary managed a staff of four people. Typically, a staff member would handle every aspect of an event, which included signing contracts, filling out forms, arranging for tours of the museum, and working with the operations, security, and janitorial departments of the museum as well as the outside caterer. The staff member would also attend the event to be sure that every-thing ran smoothly. Quite often, this became a true hands-on job, as staff members might have to roll up their sleeves and arrange chairs, hang banners, or find an extra table at the last minute. Before Hillary got this job, she was a staff member arranging events. She had also worked as a convention planner and in the development department of a children's science museum.

Job Prerequisites. To work as an event planner, Hillary says that you must be a very well-organized person who is capable of han-dling a lot of details but at the same time capable of seeing the big picture of what each event will be like. Because there are always surprises in setting up an event (the caterer may be late, you may have forgotten to order something), it is essential to be a flexible, can-do person who does not wilt under pressure. You also need to be someone who can work well with a variety of people, from corporate executives to the cleanup crew.

Corporate Jobs for Arts Lovers

Many businesses have art, archives, and artifacts of historical importance that need to be preserved, organized, and shared with the public. Researching, managing, and displaying these resources are inviting jobs for culture lovers. The number of jobs in this area, while not large, may still be greater than you imagine. For example, the Wells Fargo Bank has a variety of job opportunities in its nine museums and in the history department of the bank. Each museum presents Wells Fargo's unique role in the growth of America and its area. Visitors can see original stagecoaches, bank-ing and express documents, working telegraphs, western art, gold coins, old money, and other historical objects. The most visible artifacts of the bank are the fourteen stagecoaches. They are seen in the museums, as well as in parades and civic events. Each museum offers free educational tours for all ages, with a special emphasis complementing state primary and secondary American history curricula. The museums also tailor tours for senior groups, college students, and business professionals.

Culture lovers in this department even include stagecoach drivers. The department also manages archives that contain information about the development of the western frontier, since Wells Fargo is the oldest bank involved in financing in the West.

Culture lovers who would like to work in this type of corporate setting should have backgrounds in art, history, or education. Besides having bachelor's degrees, several of the employees in this department have advanced degrees.

Corporate Giving Jobs

Watch a symphony or an opera on PBS, and often you will see the name of a corporation as the sponsor of the program. More and more corporations are associating their companies with the arts by sponsoring festivals, television programs, and touring companies. Some even have special corporate giving departments. While there are a very limited number of jobs in this area, they can be very appealing to culture lovers. Applicants with business experience are often corporations' first choices for these positions.

Jobs with the Government

In Europe, it has always been traditional for state and city governments to support the arts. Not until 1965 and the creation of the National Endowment for the Arts (NEA) did the United States government really begin to contribute to the arts. The mission of the National Endowment for the Arts is

- to foster the excellence, diversity, and vitality of the arts in the United States; and
- to help broaden the availability and appreciation of such excellence, diversity, and vitality.

Culture lovers reading this mission statement can readily appreciate that within this independent agency of the federal government, there are many jobs for those who wish to be a part of implementing this mission. Block grants from NEA program funds are allocated to state and regional art agencies, thereby creating additional jobs for culture lovers at lower levels. In addition, even the smallest communities may have local arts commissions that can be independent or supported by the state or local government. Culture lovers can also find jobs in museums from the Smithsonian to state museums, at arts centers like the Kennedy Center, and with a variety of cultural programs.

Federal Government Jobs

With the advent of the Internet and the ability to find jobs and submit resumes or the Optional Application for Federal Employment (OF-612) online, the procedure for getting a job with the federal government is far less complicated than it once was. To better understand the process, it can still be helpful, however, to read books like the following:

Damp, Dennis V. *The Book of U.S. Government Jobs: Where They Are, What's Available, and How to Get One.* McKees Rock, PA: Brookhaven Press, 2005.

Maxwell, Bruce, ed. *A Guide to America's Federal Jobs: A Complete Directory of U.S. Government Career Opportunities.* Indianapolis, IN: JIST Works, 2005.

Troutman, Kathryn K. *Federal Resume Guidebook: Write a Winning Federal Resume to Get in, Get Promoted, and Survive in a Government Career.* Indianapolis, IN: JIST Works, 2004.

Finding a Job at the Federal Level. Your search for a job is a three-step process. Go to the Office of Personnel Management (OPM) website at www.usajobs.opm.gov. Then follow these steps:

- **Step 1: Create your account.** This allows you to create and post resumes, attract employers, and have job notices e-mailed to you.
- **Step 2: Search for jobs.** You just enter your desired job information and search the database of thousands of jobs. Then use your online resume to apply instantly.
- **Step 3: Manage your career.** Get all the information and advice online necessary to advance to a different job with the government.

Many government agencies have direct-hire authority and will hire employees without ever listing their openings with the OPM. For this reason, it is important to initiate personal contact with the cultural agencies that interest you. It is often a good idea to write or call the department heads or supervisors and speak to them directly. One publication that can assist in your job search is the *Federal Jobs Digest*. This biweekly newspaper tracks federal vacancies. It is available in some public libraries and is updated periodically at www.jobsfed.com.

Job Opportunities for Students. If you want to get a head start on an arts-related federal job as a student, visit the OPM website and you will find these opportunities:

- Presidential Management Fellows Program
- Student Educational Employment Program
- Student Career Experience Program
- Scholarship for Service Program
- summer jobs
- student jobs
- e-Scholar opportunities

Salaries. If you get an arts job with the federal government, you will probably be paid under the General Schedule (GS), which is composed of fifteen grades numbered GS-1 through GS-15. Each grade has a salary range of ten steps that is defined by the level of responsibility, type of work, and the various qualifications for each position. Employees are typically promoted through steps 1, 2, and 3 at the rate of one step per year. In steps 4, 5, and 6, they move up one step every two years. And in 7, 8, and 9, they move up one step every three years. This list shows 2006 salary figures.

TABLE 1. General Schedule: Salary Levels in the Federal Government

GRADES	STEP 1	STEP 10
1	$16,352	$20,450
2	$18,385	$23,134
3	$20,060	$26,081
4	$22,519	$29,278
5	$25,195	$32,755
6	$28,085	$36,509
7	$31,209	$40,569
8	$34,563	$44,931
9	$38,175	$49,632
10	$42,040	$54,649
11	$46,189	$60,049
12	$55,360	$71,965
13	$65,832	$85,578
14	$77,793	$101,130
15	$91,507	$118,957

Source: *Office of Personnel Management, 2006*

State Government Jobs

The individual states vary considerably in how they meet the artistic needs of their citizens. The decisions about which groups and individuals in each state receive money to support their artistic endeavors are made by commissions appointed by the governors.

The staff of the state art agencies, or councils as they may be called, usually makes recommendations to these commissions. Culture lovers with state agencies do such diverse jobs as develop arts festivals, work with schools, help grant seekers complete their forms, and write informational books and pamphlets. The typical state art agency has an executive director, a fiscal officer, an information officer, programs directors, and a grants administrator, plus administrative and clerical support staff.

At the state level, job qualifications are very specific for each open position. For example, an applicant wishing to work as a music program director would need to have a background in music. Beyond having specific skills, applicants should have the following additional skills:

- a knowledge of accounting and budgeting so they can read and understand the agency's budget
- an understanding of the importance of teamwork
- the ability to work with volunteers
- experience working on cultural activities, such as festivals and art shows

Finding a Job at the State Level. Culture lovers wanting to find positions with the government in administering arts programs can visit state employment offices, which provide lists of current employment opportunities. You may find it easier, however, to conduct an online search of your state government's website. In addition, in state and county capitals and city government offices, you will be able to pick up employment listings and view job openings on bulletin boards.

Jobs with Foundations

The J. Paul Getty Trust operates several entities in the visual arts and related humanities, including the well-known J. Paul Getty Museum, the Getty Conservation Institute, the Getty Villa in

Malibu, and the Getty Research Institute dedicated to advanced scholarship in the arts and humanities. Culture lovers interested in working for organizations that provide financial support to different arts groups can have gratifying careers working in foundations such as the Getty Trust. Unfortunately, there is considerable competition for these jobs, and many are obtained by word of mouth or networking.

Foundations are incorporated nonprofit organizations that operate by giving grants to organizations, by operating their own programs, or by a combination of awarding grants and running their own programs. Foundations are established by corporations, families, and individuals who state the purpose of the organization in the by-laws.

Some foundations are concerned solely with the arts, but many have broader interests. Small foundations may not have any paid staff or may be administered by a part-time director. Large foundations have departmentalized staffs. The larger the foundation, the better its staff members are paid.

Culture lovers who are interested in working at a foundation should visit the website of the Foundation Center to learn more about foundations. The Center's database includes information on more than seventy-eight thousand foundations, corporate giving programs, and grant-making public charities.

The Foundation Center also has five library/learning centers located in New York, Atlanta, Cleveland, San Francisco, and Washington, D.C. These centers have a core collection of Foundation Center publications. A number of libraries, community foundations, and other nonprofit resource centers also have Foundation Center publications.

The locations of all these sources of foundation information can be found on the center's website. In addition, you can find out online about all the training courses the center offers both in classrooms and online. For more information, contact:

Foundation Center
79 Fifth Avenue and Sixteenth Street
New York, NY 10003
www.fdncenter.org

Volunteers and Interns in the Arts

A great number of culture lovers, just like you, dream of finding jobs related to art, music, dance, theater, and other fine arts. The competition for even entry-level positions can be fierce in certain areas. Imagine having to have a doctorate to get certain jobs at the Smithsonian. Many positions, especially in museums, require successful applicants to have master's degrees.

Having the appropriate academic background is still not sufficient for many jobs that are extremely competitive. The edge to getting a job is often having experience, and two of the best ways to gain this experience are by serving as a volunteer or working as an intern. Volunteers and interns learn how arts organizations operate. They can discover interesting career possibilities they never knew existed. And they can perform so well in their jobs that they are offered positions where they have been volunteering or interning.

Careers for Culture Lovers

Working in careers in the arts raises the career satisfaction of culture lovers because they are refreshed from working each day with the arts they love.

> *The finest works of art are precious, among other reasons, because they make it possible for us to know, if only imperfectly and for a while, what it actually feels like to think subtly and feel nobly.*
> —Aldous Huxley, *Ends and Means XII*

About the Authors

M arjorie Eberts and Margaret Gisler have been writing professionally for twenty-five years. They are prolific freelance authors with more than eighty books in print, including twenty-one books on careers. The two authors have also written textbooks, beginning readers, study skills books for schoolchildren, and a college preparation handbook. In addition, they write Dear Teacher, a nationally syndicated education advice column for parents.

Attending cultural events is the number one avocation of these two authors. Their tastes are eclectic, ranging from attending art house films to visiting modern art museums. Writing this book was a special pleasure for the authors as it gave them the opportunity to meet so many fellow culture lovers who are bringing beauty into the lives of everyone who goes to symphonies, operas, ballets, museums, theatrical productions, and art galleries.

Eberts is a graduate of Stanford University, and Gisler is a graduate of Ball State and Butler Universities. Both received their specialist degrees in education from Butler University. Gisler recently completed a doctorate in education at Ball State University.